Dan Gookin's Guide to XML and JSON Programming

Dan Gookin's Guide to XML and JSON Programming
Written by Dan Gookin

Published by Quantum Particle Bottling Co.,
Coeur d'Alene, ID, 83814
USA

For additional information on this or other publications from Dan Gookin and Quantum Particle Bottling Co., please visit https://www.wambooli.com/

Edition 1.0
August 2019

Table of Contents

Introduction

XML and JSON are data interchange formats. They store complex data in human readable, plain text. This approach makes these formats accessible to a wide array of platforms and programming languages.

This book describes how to use freely available C language libraries to access, process, and generate XML and JSON data in your code.

Assumptions

To get the most from this book, you must be familiar with the C language and comfortable enough with your computer's development environment that you can install and configure third-party libraries. Further, you must know how to link in such libraries as well as know the header files' location.

I've managed to get both libraries installed and working with the Code::Blocks IDE in Windows. Easier is to use the Ubuntu shell in Windows 10. If you're comfortable with it, programming in a terminal window can be far nimbler than using an IDE, especially when learning something new and for the short, to-the-point examples used in this text.

If you're using Mac OS X or a Linux variation, I recommend using the terminal window. Not only will your package manager easily install the libraries, but the compiler is generally configured to find the installed libraries automatically.

I've not tested this book with XCode on the Mac. Also, I understand that Code::Blocks for the Mac has its quirks. In Windows, I'm aware that Microsoft Visual Studio has issues accessing third-party libraries.

XML and JSON Libraries

To work with XML and JSON data, you must install special libraries that extend what the C compiler can do. The two libraries I've chosen to manipulate XML and JSON data are Libxml2 and json-c.

Specifics on how these libraries are installed, configured, and tested are offered in the book's text.

Conventions

This book uses the following conventions:

C language keywords, library keywords, and function names appear in italic text, such as *printf()* and *char*.

Variable names and filenames appear in monospaced text, colored blue if color is available: `x` and `libxml2.h`.

Functions are presented in a manner similar to the man page format:

```
xmlDocPtr = xmlParseFile( char *filename );
```

Program code appears with the source filename first, followed by the code:

00-01_jsondump.c

```
1   #include <stdio.h>
2   #include <stdlib.h>
3   #include <json-c/json.h>
4
5   int main()
6   {
7       const char filename[] = "sample.json";
8       json_object *jdata;
9       const char *jstring;
10
11      jdata = json_object_from_file(filename);
12      if( jdata==NULL )
13      {
14          fprintf(stderr,"Unable to process %s\n",filename);
15          exit(1);
16      }
17
18      jstring = json_object_to_json_string(jdata);
19      puts(jstring);
20
21      return(0);
22  }
```

The source filename uses chapter number, sequence number, followed by a unique name.

The line numbers to the left of the bar are for reference only; do not type them into your code.

The demonstration programs in this book are short and to the point. As such, they rarely include comments.

Later code examples dispense with error-checking, primarily to keep the code examples short. The text points out when I omit the error-checking code, though I strongly recommend that you always check for errors in your own programs.

Some statements are split across several lines in the source code file. This approach was made to avoid ugly text-wrapping that occurs in narrow-margin reading material.

Source code, sample files, and other resources are available on the companion website:

`https://c-for-dummies.com/xmljson`

Files are available individually or can be downloaded as an archive.

Contacting the Author

Here is my email address:

`dgookin@wambooli.com`

I cannot promise to answer all email, though I don't mind saying "Hi" or addressing a programming puzzle directly tied to this book. I cannot troubleshoot your code for you, and I don't offer technical support on computer or compiler issues. Thanks for understanding.

Dan Gookin,
August 2019

1. Data Interchange Formats

To share complex data between different resources, scientists holding clipboards while wearing white lab coats have developed common data interchange formats. These formats express complex data in a consistent manner, allowing the information to be generated, shared, and read by a variety of computers, networks, and programming languages.

The two most common data interchange formats are XML and JSON.

- XML is the eXtensible Markup Language.

- JSON stands for JavaScript Object Notation.

Both formats use plain text to express complex data and both are human-readable.

Here is sample XML data:

```xml
<?xml version="1.0" encoding="UTF-8" ?>
<character>
 <firstName>Simon</firstName>
 <middleName>Bar</middleName>
 <lastName>Sinister</lastName>
 <address>
     <street>123 Evil Ave.</street>
     <city>Bigtown</city>
     <state>New York</state>
     <zip>12345</zip>
 </address>
 <isCartoon value="true" />
 <IQ>213.5</IQ>
 <phone type="lab">212 555-1234</phone>
 <phone type="mobile">868 555-1234</phone>
 <assistant>Cad Lackey</assistant>
</character>
```

Here is what JSON data looks like:

```json
{
 "firstName": "Simon",
 "middleName": "Bar",
 "lastName": "Sinister",
 "address": {
     "street": "123 Evil Ave.",
     "city": "Bigtown",
     "state": "New York",
```

```
    "zip": "12345"
},
"isCartoon": true,
"IQ": 213.5,
"phones": [
    {
        "type": "lab",
        "number": "212 555-1234"
    },
    {
        "type": "mobile",
        "number": "868 555-1234"
    }
],
"assistant": "Cad Lackey",
"spouse": null,
"favorite numbers": [ 2, 13, 23, 66 ]
}
```

Alas, neither data interchange format is natively digestible by the C programming language.

Being a mid-level programming language, C uses primitive data types: *int*, *char*, *float*, and so on. Even its complex data types, such as a structure, are limited in scope. While other languages have the chops to directly digest XML and JSON data, a C programmer must add a library to provide the functions and tools necessary.

The good news is that plenty of XML and JSON libraries are available. These libraries extend the C language's capabilities, allowing your programs to easily read, processes, and write XML and JSON data. This book explains how to install and use these libraries.

2. The XML Format

To program the XML format, you must understand how it holds data and the lingo used to describe the format's syntax.

While the XML standard uses a specific data presentation and format, the content of XML data can be anything. The *extensible* part of the name means that the user defines the data, its organization, and how it's presented.

When you encounter XML data, you also meet up with some form of documentation describing the data's contents. This is how you know what names and data types to look. For example, the data may contain a `Name` tag with a string value. The tag names used in the data are consistent, which is how you can plumb the data's depths to extract needed information.

XML is frequently compared with HTML, the formatting language used on the world wide web. XML data is not limited, however, to describing a web page.

XML data structure

XML data is organized into tags, which identify and describe data. These tags are enclosed in angle brackets, typically presented in pairs of an open tag, followed by data or value associated with the tag, and then a closing tag using the same name. Tags are described in detail later in this Chapter.

THE XML PROLOG

The first line of an XML file, or first tag presented in the data, is called the prolog. This tag states the XML version and character encoding. This tag is optional, though if it exists it always comes first, and it uses a unique tag format not found elsewhere in the document.

Here's a typical prolog tag:

```
<?xml version="1.0" encoding="UTF-8" ?>
```

The prolog tag is an empty tag; it has no end tag or data. Question marks are nestled within angle brackets. The prolog tag contains a `version` attribute plus an optional `encoding` attribute.

THE DOCUMENT ROOT

The tag immediately following the prolog, or the first tag in XML data when a prolog isn't present, is the root tag.

The root tag can contain data, though its purpose is to enclose all other tags in the document. The root tag serves as the top level in the XML data's hierarchical structure.

XML data has only one root tag. If two "root" tags are needed, they must be nested within a single tag, which is then the root.

CHILD TAGS AND SUB-CHILD TAGS

Tags nested below the root are child tags. To each other, they're sibling tags; brothers and sisters. Other than the root, each tag in the XML data features a parent tag.

Child tags can have their own child tags, cascading down in a hierarchical structure. The method depends on how the data is organized.

This parent-child-sibling relationship plays a role in how tags are accessed when programming the Libxml2 library.

XML tags

To describe, store, and transport data, XML uses tags. These tags mark elements and describe data.

Tags generally pair up, with data framed by a start and end tag pair. Tags can also be empty, lacking an end tag.

Within the tag, attributes can be expressed, further refining the data.

START AND END TAGS

A tag a single word or other non-breaking text enclosed in angle brackets, as in `<tag>`.

Most tags come in pairs, a start and end tag. Both contain the same word in the same case, though the end tag features a slash prefixing the word:

```
<name>Simon Bar Sinister</name>
```

Between the tags is the data the tags help describe. Above the *name* tag contains the string Simon Bar Sinister.

Another term for a tag pair is *element*. The data described by the element is its *value*.

EMPTY TAGS

A tag that lacks an end tag is referred to as an empty tag:

```
<item-separator />
```

This type of tag ends with the slash character before the closing angle bracket.

An empty tag can indicate a binary condition, data description, or can be augmented with attributes to further describe its purpose.

NESTED TAGS

Tags that contain other tags are referred to as nested tags. For example, the name tag below encloses three additional tags that help describe the data:

```
<name>
    <first>Simon</first>
    <middle>Bar</middle>
    <last>Sinister</last>
</name>
```

The name tag is the parent tag; first, middle, and last are child tags.

Tags can be nested as many levels deep as necessary. They must be contained within a parent tag.

TAG ATTRIBUTES

To further describe data, a tag can also contain an attribute. The attribute is a name/value pair in the format name="value".

```
<temperature scale="Celsius">16</temperature>
```

Above the *temperature* tag contains the attribute *scale*, which is set to the text `Celsius`. The closing tag need only repeat the tag name, not the attribute.

Empty tags can also contain attributes, which is another way they can describe data.

XML is extensible

When exploring XML data, keep in mind that the tag names and data are user-defined. They describe whatever is needed, providing that the rules mentioned in this chapter are followed.

To put it another way, you must know what's in the XML data before you go exploring. Not every XML file has the same elements. Do your homework before you deal with the XML data to know precisely what you're looking for.

3. The Libxml2 Library

A host of XML libraries are available for the C language. The one I use in this book is Libxml2, which is available from the http://www.xmlsoft.org website.

The library can be downloaded manually, for example to use with Code::Blocks. If you're using a terminal window, such as the Ubuntu *bash* shell in Windows 10, you can use the *apt* package manager tool to install a copy.

To obtain the library for Linux, use your distro's package manager (such as *apt*) to install and configure a copy. On the Mac, use Homebrew in the terminal to install the *libxml2* library.

When using a package manager, search for and install the libxml2-dev library.

Documentation and sample code are available on the xmlsoft website.

Installing the library

If you're using a bash shell and the *apt* package manager, type this command to search for the library:

```
sudo apt search libxml2-dev
```

Type the superuser password, then peruse the list to look for the library, which should be the only search result. For example:

```
Sorting... Done
Full Text Search... Done
libxml2-dev/bionic-updates,bionic-security,now 2.9.4+dfsg1-
6.1ubuntu1.2 amd64
  Development files for the GNOME XML library
```

The specific text you see varies, specifically the latter part of the third line. And if you see the text [installed] appended, the library is already installed and you're ready to code.

After finding the library, use *apt-get* to proceed with installation:

```
sudo apt-get libxml2-dev
```

Finding the header files

15

The libxml2 library sets its header files in the /usr/include or /usr/local/include directories. Look for a libxml directory. If you can't find this directory, look instead for the libxml2 directory, which contains the libxml directory. When this configuration is the case, you must do some fixin' to allow your programs to access the header files.

Each header file in the libxml directory assumes that the prefix directory is libxml and not libxml2/libxml. Therefore, some shell magic must occur for the header files to find each other. On my system, I aliased the install location:

/usr/include/libxml2/libxml

To this location:

/user/local/include/libxml

To perform this wizardry, in the /usr/local/include directory type this command:

```
sudo ln -s /usr /include/libxml2/libxml
```

By creating this symbolic link, the header files can find each other.

For a manual installation, take note of the library's include and lib folders. You must specify these folders in an IDE so that the header files and library can be included and linked into your code. See the later section, "Building the code in an IDE."

Testing the installation (terminal)

The code presented in the listing 03-01_xmltest.c tests the Libxml2 library's installation. The output is the library version number.

03-01_xmltest.c

```
1  #include <stdio.h>
2  #include <libxml/xmlversion.h>
3
4  int main()
5  {
6      printf("libxml2 version %d\n",LIBXML_VERSION);
7
8      return(0);
9  }
```

The header file, xmlversion.h, is included at Line 2. It contains the defined constant LIBXML_VERSION. This constant is output by the *printf()* statement at Line 6.

To compile this code, ensure that you link in the Libxml2 library. The library isn't required as the code lacks any of its functions. The reason for linking in the library is to ensure that it's been properly installed.

Here's the command I use in the same directory that contains the source code file, 03-01_xmltest.c:

```
clang -lxml2 03-01_xmltest.c
```

clang is the name of the compiler, though you can use *gcc* or *cc* or whatever your favorite compiler might be.

To link in the Libxml2 library use the **-lxml2** switch. It's a lowercase L followed by the library name, xml2.

♦ *If the program doesn't compile, specify the -l switch as the last item after the source code filename.*

Finally comes the source code filename: 03-01_xmltest.c.

Upon success, the output file generated is the default, a.out. To run this program, type:

```
./a.out
```

The library's version number is output.

All XML sample code presented in this book is compiled and run in the same manner. The commands are similar, with the difference of the source code filename. Source code for this book, as well as sample files, are available on the companion website: https://c-for-dummies.com/xmljson/

Building the code in an IDE

If you manually install the Libxml2 library, you can use an IDE to build and run the sample programs. I've not tested every IDE and I'm aware that some are averse to including third-party libraries.

In Code::Blocks, to create programs that link in the Libxml2 library you must create a new C language console application project. After doing so, specify the path to both the Libxml2 library file as well as the directory (folder) where the header files are kept.

After creating a new console application for C, follow these steps to ensure that the Libxml2 library and header files can be accessed to create the program:

1. Choose Project, Build Options.

2. In the Project Build Options dialog box, click the Linker Settings tab.

3. Use the Add button to add the libxml2 library file to the project.

The library is named `libxml2.lib`. You must brows to the folder containing this file. I recommend referencing this file by using an absolute (not relative) path.

4. After setting the link library, click the Search Directories tab in the Project Build Options dialog box.

5. Click the Add button.

6. Browse to the `include` folder downloaded with the Libxml2 library archive.

Set the `include` folder, not `libxml`. This way your project's source code files can find the library's headers.

7. Click OK to close the various dialog boxes.

You can now build the Code::Blocks project and incorporate information from the Libxml2 library file and headers.

4. Basic XML Reading

The C language doesn't natively generate or process XML data. Therefore, whatever information your code is trying to access is either stored in a buffer or dwells in a file. Either way, the Libxml2 library offers functions to access both types of data.

Understanding libxml2's philosophy

Before getting too far down the road, it's important that you understand how the Libxml2 library goes about presenting XML data. Knowing its philosophy now helps avoid becoming frustrated later.

DEFINED VARIABLES

The Libxml2 library uses special variables to access XML data. These variables often represent structures that store the data. The variables are typedefs to the structures as well as other data types, defined in the various header files, such as `parser.h`.

The most important Libxml2 variable is *xmlDocPtr*. Think of this variable as a file handle. XML data can be read from a file or memory and the result is referenced through an *xmlDocPtr* variable.

♦ *I use the* xmlDocPtr *data type in my code. This variable is the defined pointer version of the* xmlDoc *data type. The difference is that for* xmlDoc, *the variable must be declared as a pointer, as in* `xmlDoc *doc;`

The *xmlDocPtr* variable represents the XML data throughout your code. Other Libxml2 functions use the variable to reference the data as a whole. This variable is also used to clean up when you're done examining, manipulating, or creating XML data.

A second important variable is the *xmlNodePtr*. This variable references elements within an XML document. These elements or nodes are what store the data kept in the XML format.

♦ *As with* xmlDoctPtr, *the* xmlNodePtr *variable is the pointer-defined version of the* xmlNode *variable.*

Other special variables are used as well, such as *xmlChar* to identify strings within a node.

The `xmlsoft.org` website provides full documentation for these variables, as well as all the functions required to read and manipulate XML data.

DATA REPRESENTATION

If you understand how linked lists work in C, you have a clue as to how the Libxml2 library references XML data. It helps to think of elements within the data as structures with pointers that reference other elements.

For example, all elements at the same (peer) level in XML data are linked to each other:

```
<beverage>Orange Juice</beverage>
<protein>Bacon</protein>
<sweet>Banana</sweet>
```

Above, `beverage` is the first item in an *xmlNodePtr* list. To access the next element, the *next* member of its structure is accessed – just like a linked list. If the *xmlNodePtr* variable is named `node`, the statement to browse elements looks like this:

```
node = node->next
```

The last item in the list has a *next* member value of `NULL`. This is how you can tell you've reached the last sibling in a clutch of elements.

Similarly, elements with children have a *children* member that references an *xmlNodePtr* variable representing the first child element. The *parent* element helps navigate back to the next-higher element, or node, in the data.

Accessing XML data in memory

Suppose your code obtained XML data from a website and stored it in memory. It sits in a character buffer, like a string of text. Your task is to use the Libxml2 library to access the data.

THE MEMORY PARSER

To access that data, use the *xmlParseMemory()* function. It has this format:

```
xmlDocPtr xmlParseMemory(const char *buffer, int size);
```

The first argument is a buffer or string containing the XML data. The second argument is the buffer's size.

The value returned in an *xmlDocPtr* variable. This variable is used throughout the rest of the code to access the elements in the data.

When you're done processing the XML data, the *xmlFreeDoc()* function releases any memory allocated and assigned to the *xmlDocPtr* variable (a structure). This function's sole argument is the *xmlDocPtr* variable.

The following code demonstrates how the *xmlParseMemory()* function works, how the *xmlDocPtr* variable is used, and shows the *xmlFreeDoc()* function's use after the operation is complete.

04-01_xmlmem1.c

```
1   #include <stdio.h>
2   #include <stdlib.h>
3   #include <libxml/parser.h>
4
5   int main()
6   {
7       const char data[] = "<rootNode>\
8                           <child>Baby1</child>\
9                           </rootNode>";
10      xmlDocPtr doc;
11
12      doc = xmlParseMemory( data, sizeof(data) );
13      if( doc==NULL)
14      {
15          fprintf(stderr,"Unable to parse data\n");
16          xmlFreeDoc(doc);
17          exit(1);
18      }
19      puts("Data parsed successfully");
20
21      xmlFreeDoc(doc);
22
23      return(0);
24  }
```

The XML data is stored in a string `data` declared between Lines 7 and 9. An *xmlDocPtr* variable `doc` is declared at Line 10.

The `data` string is parsed by the *xmlParseMemory()* function at Line 12. Upon success an *xmlDocPtr* variable is returned, stored in variable `doc`.

Upon failure, NULL is returned. If so, an error message output, the *xmlDocPtr* variable is freed, and the program exits.

Here's sample output:

```
Data parsed successfully
```

THE ROOT ELEMENT

Most often, the first step after creating an *xmlDocPtr* variable to parse XML data is to read the document's root element. The function that extracts this data is *xmlDocGetRootElement()*. Its sole argument is the *xmlDocPtr* representing the XML data to parse:

```
root = xmlDocGetRootElement(doc);
```

The value returned from *xmlDocGetRootElement()* is a *xmlNodePtr* variable representing the root element. If the function fails, such as the data lacks a root element, NULL is returned.

The following code is an update to 04-01_xmlmem1.c. This update reads the root node and displays the root element's name, referenced by the *name* member of the *xmlNotePtr* structure returned.

04-02_xmlmem2.c

```
1   #include <stdio.h>
2   #include <stdlib.h>
3   #include <libxml/parser.h>
4
5   int main()
6   {
7       const char data[] = "<rootNode>\
8                       <child>Baby1</child>\
9                       </rootNode>";
10      xmlDocPtr doc;
11      xmlNodePtr root;
12
13      doc = xmlParseMemory( data, sizeof(data) );
14
15      root = xmlDocGetRootElement(doc);
16      if( root==NULL)
17      {
18          fprintf(stderr,"Can't read data\n");
19          xmlFreeDoc(doc);
20          exit(1);
21      }
22      printf("Root node is '%s'\n",root->name);
23
24      xmlFreeDoc(doc);
25
26      return(0);
27  }
```

Line 13 extracts the *xmlDocPtr* variable doc from the data stored in buffer data. This variable should be compared against the NULL constant to ensure that the function properly parsed the data; I've removed the error-checking here for brevity's sake.

Line 15 uses the *xmlDocGetRootElement()* function, which returns an *xmlNodePtr* value stored in variable root. This value is immediately tested at Line 16 to determine success.

Upon success, at Line 22, the root node's name is output, as in:

```
Root node is 'rootNode'
```

Reading XML data from a file

The Libxml2 function that reads XML data from a file is *xmlParseFile()*. Its argument is a string, the name of the file to open. Upon success, the file is opened, read, and closed. The parsed XML data is referenced by an *xmlDocPtr* value returned from the function:

```
doc = xmlParseFile(filename);
```

Upon failure, the function returns NULL. I strongly recommend this condition always be tested. (Other functions I skip testing in this book, such as *xmlDocGetRootElement()*, though these should be tested in practice.)

04-03_xmlfile.c

```
1   #include <stdio.h>
2   #include <stdlib.h>
3   #include <libxml/parser.h>
4
5   int main()
6   {
7       const char filename[] = "sample.xml";
8       xmlDocPtr doc;
9       xmlNodePtr root;
10
11      doc = xmlParseFile(filename);
12      if( doc==NULL )
13      {
14          fprintf(stderr,"Unable to process %s\n",filename);
15          exit(1);
16      }
17
18      root = xmlDocGetRootElement(doc);
19      printf("Root node is '%s'\n",root->name);
20
21      xmlFreeDoc(doc);
```

```
22
23        return(0);
24    }
```

The sample file referenced at Line 7 is available for download on the companion website. The filename is used as an argument for the *xmlParseFile()* function at Line 11, its value returned in *xmlDocPtr* variable doc. This variable is immediately tested against NULL to ensure success opening and processing the XML file.

The remainder of the code is similar to the earlier example 04-02_xmlmem2.c: the root node is fetched and its name output:

Here is sample output:

```
Root node is 'character'
```

Reading the XML prolog

If prolog information is present in the XML data, it can be accessed from the *xmlDocPtr* variable. The version and encoding items are available as members of the structure returned. The version is a string held in the *version* member; the *encoding* string holds the encoding string.

04-04_xmlprolog.c

```
1    #include <stdio.h>
2    #include <stdlib.h>
3    #include <libxml/parser.h>
4
5    int main()
6    {
7        const char filename[] = "sample.xml";
8        xmlDocPtr doc;
9
10       doc = xmlParseFile(filename);
11       if( doc==NULL )
12       {
13           fprintf(stderr,"Unable to process %s\n",filename);
14           exit(1);
15       }
16       printf("XML version is %s\n",doc->version);
17       printf("XML encoding is %s\n",doc->encoding);
18
19       xmlFreeDoc(doc);
20
21       return(0);
22    }
```

Lines 16 and 17 output the version and encoding information available in the `sample.xml` file's prolog. These items are members of the structure returned and available in the *xmlDocPtr* variable `doc`. This variable is a pointer, which is why pointer structure member notation is used.

Here's sample output:

```
XML version is 1.0
XML encoding is UTF-8
```

If the prolog isn't available, NULL values are stored for the *version* and *encoding* members. When using these items in your code, ensure that you check for the NULL conditions.

5. XML Spelunking

Exploring XML data starts by using the *xmlDocGetRootElement()* function to extract the root node. Once you obtain this value, saved in an *xmlNotePtr* variable, you examine the node's children – the next level of elements in the data.

The child elements can have sibling elements, creating a level within the hierarchical structure of the data. These elements may also have children, which adds to the complexity of the data but keeps information organized.

Processing the top-level

All properly formed XML data has a top-level or root element accessed by using the *xmlDocGetRootElement()* function. Upon success, this function returns an *xmlNodePtr* variable. From this structure variable, the *children* member points to the next-level element.

DOES THE ROOT HAVE CHILDREN?

After obtaining the root node variable, confirm that child elements are present by testing the *children* structure member against NULL. When the value of `root->children` (where `root` is the root *xmlNodePtr* variable name) isn't NULL, an *if* test returns true, as demonstrated in this code:

05-01_rootchildren.c

```
1   #include <stdio.h>
2   #include <stdlib.h>
3   #include <libxml/parser.h>
4
5   int main()
6   {
7       const char filename[] = "sample.xml";
8       xmlDocPtr doc;
9       xmlNodePtr root;
10
11      doc = xmlParseFile(filename);
12      if( doc==NULL )
13      {
14          fprintf(stderr,"Unable to open %s\n",filename);
15          exit(1);
16      }
```

```
17
18      root = xmlDocGetRootElement(doc);
19      if( root->children )
20          puts("The root node has children!");
21      else
22          puts("No children are available!");
23
24      xmlFreeDoc(doc);
25
26      return(0);
27  }
```

At Line 18, the root node is obtained and stored in *xmlNodePtr* variable `root`.

Line 19 confirms that the root node has children: if the `root->children` variable isn't `NULL`, the first *puts()* statement is executed at Line 20, otherwise Line 22 is executed.

When processing the `sample.xml` file, children are present. The output is:

`The root node has children!`

CHILD ELEMENT VISITATION

To access the root node's children, and eventually explore all XML data, you must save the root's *children* member (a pointer) in another *xmlNodePtr* variable.

For example, if the root node is referenced by *xmlNodePtr* variable `root`, you save the *children* member by using the following statement:

`node = root->children;`

Variable `node` is another *xmlNodePtr* variable, from which the root's children can be accessed. Specifically, variable `node` references the first child element of the root node. This child node's name is accessed from the *name* member of the *xmlNodePtr* variable's structure, as in `node->name`.

To access the next sibling element, the *next* member of the variable's structure is accessed, as in:

`node = node->next;`

Yes, the *xmlNodePtr* variable `node` can be re-used, just as a pointer can be re-used when processing a linked list. After the above statement is executed, variable `node` references details for the next element (node) in the list.

To ensure that an element node is accessed, check the *type* member of the *xmlNodePtr* structure. The *type* member's value must be compared with the XML_ELEMENT_NODE defined constant:

```
if( node->type==XML_ELEMENT_NODE )
```

When the type member matches the XML_ELEMENT_NODE constant, you can examine the structure's other members to gather information about the element.

♦ *Some items in the list of nodes describe other attributes of the XML data, so you must ensure your code is referencing an element and not the other types of data.*

Finally, as with a linked list, the last element's *next* member is NULL. This value can be used as a condition in a loop to march though all sibling elements, as demonstrated in the following code.

05-02_topnodes.c

```
1   #include <stdio.h>
2   #include <stdlib.h>
3   #include <libxml/parser.h>
4
5   int main()
6   {
7       const char filename[] = "sample.xml";
8       xmlDocPtr doc;
9       xmlNodePtr root,node;
10
11      doc = xmlParseFile(filename);
12      if( doc==NULL )
13      {
14          fprintf(stderr,"Unable to open %s\n",filename);
15          exit(1);
16      }
17
18      root = xmlDocGetRootElement(doc);
19      for( node=root->children; node; node=node->next )
20      {
21          if( node->type==XML_ELEMENT_NODE )
22              printf("%s\n",node->name);
23      }
24
25      xmlFreeDoc(doc);
26
27      return(0);
28  }
```

Line 18 obtains the root node, stored in the root variable. In Line 19, the *for* loop processes the sibling nodes (top-level elements) like a linked list:

- The initialization `node=root->children` sets the `node` variable to the first item in the list.

- The end condition is the `node` variable itself. When this variable is `NULL`, the list has ended, and the loop can stop.

- The stepping condition is `node=node->next`, which access the next node or sibling element in the data.

At Line 21, if the node is a standard element, Line 22 outputs the node's name.

Here's sample output:

```
firstName
middleName
lastName
address
isCartoon
IQ
phone
phone
assistant
```

Dumping all the elements

To traverse through all elements in XML data, you must check to see whether any given node has children. If so, the children must be processed. The method at this point becomes recursive, with children nodes processed to look for additional children nodes on down the rabbit hole.

A RECURSIVE FUNCTION

The following code is a modification of `05-02_topnodes.c`, where the exploratory *for* loop statements have been separated into a function, *dump_elements()*, for recursive processing.

05-03_allnodes1.c

```
1   #include <stdio.h>
2   #include <stdlib.h>
3   #include <libxml/parser.h>
4
5   void dump_elements(xmlNodePtr n)
6   {
7       xmlNodePtr node;
8
9       for( node=n; node; node=node->next )
10      {
11          if( node->type==XML_ELEMENT_NODE )
```

```
12                     printf("%s\n",node->name);
13              if( node->children )
14                  dump_elements(node->children);
15          }
16  }
17
18  int main()
19  {
20      const char filename[] = "sample.xml";
21      xmlDocPtr doc;
22      xmlNodePtr root;
23
24      doc = xmlParseFile(filename);
25      if( doc==NULL )
26      {
27          fprintf(stderr,"Unable to open %s\n",filename);
28          exit(1);
29      }
30
31      root = xmlDocGetRootElement(doc);
32      dump_elements(root);
33
34      xmlFreeDoc(doc);
35
36      return(0);
37  }
```

The *dump_elements()* function at Line 5 processes sibling-level nodes in XML data. Its argument n is the parent node, such as the root node passed at Line 32.

The *for* loop at Line 9 processes all peer-level nodes. Lines 11 and 12 output the element name.

At Line 13, a test is made to determine if the children member isn't NULL. If so, the function recursively calls itself to process those child nodes. Otherwise, the *for* loop keeps spinning.

Here's sample output:

```
character
firstName
middleName
lastName
address
street
city
state
zip
isCartoon
IQ
phone
phone
assistant
```

The output includes the sub-elements of the <address> element.

A RECURSIVE FUNCTION WITH INDENTATION

The output from 05-03_allnodes1.c is rather plain. In the following update, I added indentation to the *dump_elements()* function. Otherwise, the code is the same.

05-04_allnodes2.c

```
1   #include <stdio.h>
2   #include <stdlib.h>
3   #include <libxml/parser.h>
4
5   void dump_elements(xmlNodePtr n,int i)
6   {
7       xmlNodePtr node;
8       int x;
9
10      for( node=n; node; node=node->next )
11      {
12          if( node->type==XML_ELEMENT_NODE )
13          {
14              for( x=0; x<i; x++ )
15                  putchar('\t');
16              printf("%s\n",node->name);
17          }
18          if( node->children )
19              dump_elements(node->children,i+1);
20      }
21  }
22
23  int main()
24  {
25      const char filename[] = "sample.xml";
26      xmlDocPtr doc;
27      xmlNodePtr root;
28
29      doc = xmlParseFile(filename);
30      if( doc==NULL )
31      {
32          fprintf(stderr,"Unable to open %s\n",filename);
33          exit(1);
34      }
35
36      root = xmlDocGetRootElement(doc);
37      dump_elements(root,0);
38
39      xmlFreeDoc(doc);
30
41      return(0);
42  }
```

The addition of *int* argument i to the function's declaration allows a *for* loop (Line 10) to generate tabs. The indentation is equal to the level of recursion; each time the function calls itself (at Line 19), the value of variable i is increased by one.

Here's sample output:

```
character
        firstName
        middleName
        lastName
        address
                street
                city
                state
                zip
        isCartoon
        IQ
        phone
        phone
        assistant
```

Finding a specific element

To hunt for a specific node, you must be familiar with the structure of the XML document you're examining. Remember, the data is extensible, so an assumption is made that you know what to look for.

From the `sample.xml` file, the following code hunts for the `<lastName>` element. To find this text, you must use the *xmlStrcmp()* function, which is analogous to the *strcmp()* function in the standard C library:

```
xmlStrcmp( node->name, (const xmlChar *)"lastName")
```

The *xmlStrcmp()* function requires two arguments, both of the *xmlChar* type. When using a string literal, you must typecast it with `(const xmlChar *)` or the compiler complains.

The value returned from *xmlStrcmp()* is the same as for the *strcmp()* function, an *int* representing how the strings compare. Importantly, zero is returned when both strings match. Therefore, you often see the *xmlStrcmp()* function negated when used as a condition:

```
if ( !xmlStrcmp( node->name, (const xmlChar *)"test")
```

The `!` (not) above reverses the zero value returned by *xmlStrcmp()* if `node->name` matches the string `"test"`.

05-05_nodehunt.c

```
1   #include <stdio.h>
2   #include <stdlib.h>
3   #include <libxml/parser.h>
```

```
 4
 5   #ifndef TRUE
 6   #define TRUE 1
 7   #endif
 8   #ifndef FALSE
 9   #define FALSE 0
10   #endif
11
12   xmlNodePtr found;
13
14   int node_hunt(xmlNodePtr n, const xmlChar *e)
15   {
16       xmlNodePtr node;
17       int r;
18
19       for( node=n; node; node=node->next)
20       {
21           if( node->type==XML_ELEMENT_NODE )
22           {
23               if( !xmlStrcmp( node->name, e) )
24               {
25                   found = node;
26                   return(TRUE);
27               }
28           }
29           if( node->children )
30           {
31               r = node_hunt( node->children, e );
32               if( r )
33                   return(r);
34           }
35       }
36       return(FALSE);
37   }
38
39   int main()
40   {
41       const char filename[] = "sample.xml";
42       xmlDocPtr doc;
43       xmlNodePtr root;
44       int r;
45
46       doc = xmlParseFile(filename);
47       if( doc==NULL )
48       {
49           fprintf(stderr,"Unable to open %s\n",filename);
50           exit(1);
51       }
52
53       root = xmlDocGetRootElement(doc);
54       r = node_hunt(root, (const xmlChar *)"lastName");
55       if( r )
56       {
57           printf("<%s> found\n",found->name);
58           printf("Parent is <%s>\n",found->parent->name);
59       }
60
61       xmlFreeDoc(doc);
```

```
62
63        return(0);
64   }
```

In this code, variable found is declared externally, a "global" variable at Line 12. I'm reluctant to code this way, but given the recursive nature of the *node_hunt()* function, it's a valid solution.

The *node_hunt()* function at Line 14 has two arguments: *xmlNodePtr n*, which is where element spelunking starts, and *const xmlChar e*, representing the element name to find.

A *for* loop traverses the nodes, searching for the node->type XML_ELEMENT_NODE. If found, the *xmlStrcmp()* function is used at Line 23. Upon success, variable found is assigned the matching node and TRUE is returned.

The *if* test at Line 29 recursively calls the *node_hunt()* function to scan for child elements. It checks the return value at Line 32 to recursively return a TRUE or FALSE result.

Within the *main()* function, the root node is obtained at Line 53. Line 54 calls the *node_hunt()* function to kick off the action.

Line 55 tests the return value of *node_hunt()*. If true, the node name is output, as well as its parent name.

Here's a sample run:

```
<lastName> found
Parent is <character>
```

The *node_hunt()* function isn't without a flaw: If two or more elements share the same name, even at different levels, the function returns only the first one found.

One way to remedy this flaw is to code the hunt to find the parent element first, then searching for the child. Or if multiple children share a name, code the function to find each successive one. Your code must match the organization of the XML data for such a search to be successful.

6. Element Values and Attributes

The treasure found in XML data isn't in the elements but rather in the values. Once you find an element, the next step is to extract its value and do whatever important task is necessary to complete your program's mission.

Values in XML data are expressed between the elements but can also be found in attributes. The first step to extracting either type of data is to locate the element by name, then the fun begins.

Extracting an element's value

To extract an element's value you must first locate the element, as demonstrated at the end of the preceding Chapter. After locating that element, or node, use the *xmlNodeListGetString()* function to extract the node's contents. This function requires three arguments:

- The *xmlDocPtr* variable for the document

- The current node's children member, required because an element's contents are considered a child to the element

- The value 1 to direct the function to return the element's contents

Here's a sample statement:

```
value = xmlNodeListGetString(doc,node->children,1);
```

The value returned by *xmlNodeListGetString()* is an *xmlChar* pointer referencing the value as a string. Above, the function acts upon data referenced by variable `node`. The address returned is stored in *xmlChar* pointer variable `value`.

When you're done using pointer returned from the *xmlNodeListGetString()* function, you must use the *xmlFree()* function on the *xmlChar* variable to release its memory:

```
xmlFree(value);
```

The argument for the *xmlFree()* function is an *xmlChar* pointer, such as `value` above.

Top-Level Element Extraction

In the following source code example, the contents of the
`<lastName>` element are output. This element is right below the
root level in the sample file. This organization is assumed in the
code, which is written specifically to extract the value of the
`<lastName>` element.

06-01_nodevalue1.c

```
1    #include <stdio.h>
2    #include <stdlib.h>
3    #include <libxml/parser.h>
4
5    int main()
6    {
7        const char filename[] = "sample.xml";
8        xmlDocPtr doc;
9        xmlNodePtr root,node;
10       xmlChar *value;
11
12       doc = xmlParseFile(filename);
13       if( doc==NULL )
14       {
15           fprintf(stderr,"Unable to open %s\n",filename);
16           exit(1);
17       }
18
19       root = xmlDocGetRootElement(doc);
20       node = root->children;
21       while( node!=NULL )
22       {
23           if( !xmlStrcmp(node->name,(const xmlChar *)"lastName"))
24           {
25               value = xmlNodeListGetString(doc,node->children,1);
26               printf("Value of <%s> is '%s'\n",node->name,value);
27               xmlFree(value);
28               break;
29           }
30           node = node->next;
31       }
32
33       xmlFreeDoc(doc);
34
35       return(0);
36   }
```

Line 19 obtains the root node, saving it in *xmlNodePtr* variable
`root`. The top-level elements are accessed at Line 20 by reading
the root node's children: `node=root->children`.

A *while* loop at Line 21 processes all top-level nodes. If the
xmlStrcmp() function rings true at Line 23, the

xmlNodeListGetString() function at Line 25 extracts the node's contents, saving it in *xmlChar* variable `value`.

Line 26 outputs the string `value`. Line 27 frees the memory allocated for the string. And Line 28 breaks the *while* loop.

Here's sample output:

```
Value of <lastName> is 'Sinister'
```

CHILD-LEVEL ELEMENT EXTRACTION

In the `sample.xml` file, the `<address>` tag features sub-tags to describe the address: `<street>`, `<city>`, `<state>`, and `<zip>`. To extract the value of one of these tags, your code must first hunt down `<address>` first, and then search for the sub-tag, such as `<street>`.

The source code for this solution is found in `06-02_nodevalue2.c` below, which is a modification of the code from `06-01_nodevalue1.c`.

06-02_nodevalue2.c

```
1    #include <stdio.h>
2    #include <stdlib.h>
3    #include <libxml/parser.h>
4
5    int main()
6    {
7        const char filename[] = "sample.xml";
8        xmlDocPtr doc;
9        xmlNodePtr root,node,cnode;
10       xmlChar *value;
11
12       doc = xmlParseFile(filename);
13       if( doc==NULL )
14       {
15           fprintf(stderr,"Unable to open %s\n",filename);
16           exit(1);
17       }
18
19       root = xmlDocGetRootElement(doc);
20       node = root->children;
21       while( node!=NULL )
22       {
23           if( !xmlStrcmp(node->name,(const xmlChar *)"address"))
24           {
25               cnode = node->children;
26               while( cnode!=NULL )
27               {
28                   if( !xmlStrcmp(
29                           cnode->name,
30                           (const xmlChar *)"street")
```

```
31                       )
32                    {
33                value = xmlNodeListGetString(
34                        doc,
35                        cnode->children,
36                        1
37                        );
38                printf("Value of <%s> is '%s'\n",
39                        cnode->name,
40                        value
41                    );
42                xmlFree(value);
43                break;
44            }
45            cnode = cnode->next;
46        }
47        break;
48    }
49    node = node->next;
50   }
51
52   xmlFreeDoc(doc);
53
54   return(0);
55 }
```

The major changes from 06-01_nodevalue1.c are the addition of the *xmlNodePtr* variable cnode at Line 9, and the nested *while* loops starting at Line 21.

To make the code wrap in this book, I split several statements across multiple lines, which isn't necessary in your own code:

- At Line 28, the *xmlStrcmp()* function in the *if* condition is split to Line 31.

- At Line 33, the first statement belonging to *if*, *xmlNodeListGetString()*, is split to Line 37.

- At Line 38, the *printf()* function is split to Line 41.

Splitting the statements in this manner doesn't alter the code's execution.

When the <address> element is found at Line 23, the cnode variable is assigned to the children of the top-level element, held in node (Line 25).

A second *while* loop (Line 26) processes these children, using the *xmlStrcmp()* function to locate the <street> element at Line 28 (through Line 31). When found, the *xmlNodeListGetString()* function at Line 33 (through Line 37) extracts the element's string value and stores it in *xmlChar* variable value.

The *printf()* statement outputs the value, then variable `value` is freed with the *xmlFree()* function, at Line 38 (through Line 41).

Here's a sample run:

```
Value of <street> is '123 Evil Ave.'
```

A BETTER, RECURSIVE ELEMENT HUNT

The example from the preceding section works. It's specific to the contents of the `sample.xml` file, but it's just ugly.

A more elegant solution is to create a recursive function that plows the depths of any XML data, drilling down the various levels to find the value of a given element. Such as function is *ehunt()*, demonstrated in the following code.

06_03-nodevalue3.c

```
1   #include <stdio.h>
2   #include <stdlib.h>
3   #include <libxml/parser.h>
4
5   void ehunt(xmlDocPtr d,xmlNodePtr n,const xmlChar *c)
6   {
7       xmlNodePtr cur;
8       xmlChar *value;
9
10      for(cur=n; cur; cur=cur->next)
11      {
12          if( !xmlStrcmp(cur->name,c) )
13          {
14              value = xmlNodeListGetString(d,cur->children,1);
15              printf("<%s> is '%s'\n",cur->name,value);
16              xmlFree(value);
17              return;
18          }
19          if( cur->children )
20              ehunt(d,cur->children,c);
21      }
22  }
23
24  int main()
25  {
26      const char filename[] = "sample.xml";
27      xmlDocPtr doc;
28      xmlNodePtr root;
29
30      doc = xmlParseFile(filename);
31      if( doc==NULL )
32      {
33          fprintf(stderr,"Unable to open %s\n",filename);
34          exit(1);
35      }
36
```

```
37      root = xmlDocGetRootElement(doc);
38      ehunt(doc,root,(const xmlChar *)"assistant");
39
40      xmlFreeDoc(doc);
41
42      return(0);
43  }
```

The *ehunt()* function at Line 5 swallows three arguments:

- A *xmlDocPtr* d, representing the XML data

- An *xmlNodePtr* n, representing the first peer node in a "linked list" of elements

- A string c holding the name of the element to search for. This string must be of the *xmlChar* data type.

Everything within the *ehunt()* function should be familiar to you if you studied the code presented earlier in this Chapter. The function is recursive, calling itself when child elements are present at Lines 19 and 20. Further, once a matching string is found, the function returns at Line 17, not wasting any time.

Sample output:

```
<assistant> is 'Cad Lackey'
```

Because this code is recursive and scans all the data, you modify Line 38 to search for any valid element name in the data and have the program output its value.

Obtaining element attributes

To fetch the contents of attributes in certain tags, the *xmlGetProp()* function is used. It has two arguments: the *xmlNodePtr* variable of an element and an *xmlChar* string representing the attribute's name:

```
attrib = xmlGetProp( node, (const xmlChar *)"status" );
```

Above, the status property of the element represented by node is returned into *xmlChar* variable attrib.

After doing whatever with the text returned, you must free the *xmlChar* pointer returned by the *xmlGetProp()* function. Use the *xmlFree()* function to accomplish this task:

```
xmlFree(attrib);
```

Like other XML functions, it's assumed that you know the attribute name before you search. In the following code, the name is supplied to the *get_attrib()* function. This function recursively plows through the XML data until it finds an element with the named attribute, then it outputs the attribute's value.

06-04_attributes.c

```
1   #include <stdio.h>
2   #include <stdlib.h>
3   #include <libxml/parser.h>
4
5   void get_attrib(xmlNodePtr n,const xmlChar *a)
6   {
7       xmlNodePtr cur;
8       xmlChar *attrib;
9
10      for(cur=n; cur; cur=cur->next)
11      {
12          if( cur->type==XML_ELEMENT_NODE )
13          {
14              attrib = xmlGetProp(cur,a);
15              if( attrib!=NULL )
16                  printf("<%s> has '%s' attribute: %s\n",
17                          cur->name,
18                          a,
19                          attrib
20                          );
21              xmlFree(attrib);
22              if( cur->children )
23                  get_attrib(cur->children,a);
24          }
25      }
26  }
27
28  int main()
29  {
30      const char filename[] = "sample.xml";
31      xmlDocPtr doc;
32      xmlNodePtr root;
33
34      doc = xmlParseFile(filename);
35      if( doc==NULL )
36      {
37          fprintf(stderr,"Unable to open %s\n",filename);
38          exit(1);
39      }
40
41      root = xmlDocGetRootElement(doc);
42      get_attrib(root,(const xmlChar *)"type");
43
44      xmlFreeDoc(doc);
45
46      return(0);
47  }
```

At Line 14 in the code, the *xmlGetProp()* function grabs the attribute represented by *xmlChar* string a from the current element. The next line tests to see whether the attribute exists. If so, the element, attribute name, and its value are output.

The attribute returned is freed at Line 21. At Line 22 the element is checked for children and, if so, the function is recursively called.

Here's sample output:

```
<phone> has 'type' attribute: lab
<phone> has 'type' attribute: mobile
```

This code doesn't deal with elements that have multiple attributes. Again, if the XML data specifies multiple attributes, you can modify the code so that the two or more attributes are plucked out as necessary.

7. XML Data from Scratch

The Libxml2 library can spawn new XML data from nothing, adding it to an existing document or building new elements and their contents from scratch.

To create new XML data, start with a new *xmlDocPtr* variable, which acts as a container for the data. From then you add a root node and child nodes. Once created, the new XML data can be transferred to a buffer, sent to standard output, or saved to a file.

Creating new XML data

The minimum XML data is merely an initialized *xmlDocPtr* variable. It need not contain a root element or any other elements; it's just an empty XML document primed for action.

The function that creates a new *xmlDocPtr* variable is *xmlNewDoc()*. Its single argument is an *xmlChar* string representing the XML version number, "1.0".

After creation, you can use the *xmlSaveFormatFile()* function to send the XML data (brief as it is) to a file or to standard output. This function's format requires three arguments:

- The filename, which is created, written to, and closed upon success. The string "-" can be specified to send the data to standard output.

- The *xmlDocPtr* variable, the one returned from the *xmlNewDoc()* function

- A format value of 1 or 0, with 1 specifying formatted (indented) output

The following code demonstrates how this operation works.

07-01_newxml1.c

```
1   #include <stdio.h>
2   #include <stdlib.h>
3   #include <libxml/parser.h>
4
5   int main()
6   {
7       xmlDocPtr doc;
8
```

```
 9      doc = xmlNewDoc( (const xmlChar *)"1.0");
10      xmlSaveFormatFile( "-", doc, 0 );
11
12      xmlFreeDoc(doc);
13
14      return(0);
15  }
```

The *xmlNewDoc()* statement at Line 9 builds a new, empty chunk of XML data. The *xmlSaveFormatFile()* function at Line 10 sends the data to standard output. Here's what it looks like:

```
<?xml version="1.0"?>
```

The next step in building the data is to add the root element.

Adding the root node

XML data has a root node, a single element that contains all other data. To add a root node to an XML document, specifically a new XML document created by using *xmlNewDoc()*, you must first create a node and second assign that new node as the root.

To create a new node, the *xmlNewDocNode()* function is used. This function has four arguments:

- The *xmlDocPtr* variable representing the data where the new node is to be created

- The namespace, if any, or NULL

- An *xmlChar* string representing the element name, the name of the new node

- An *xmlChar* string representing the contents of the new node, which should be NULL for a root node

The value returned by *xmlNewDocNode()* is an *xmlNodePtr* value representing the new node. If the function fails, NULL is returned.

After creating the new node, use the *xmlDocSetRootElement()* function to assign the new node as the document's root. This function has two arguments: the *xmlDocPtr* variable representing the so-far empty XML data and the *xmlNodePtr* value returned from the *xmlNewDocNode()* function.

The following code builds upon the example presented in 07-01_newxml1.c, adding two statements to create the new node and set it as the root:

07-02_newxml2.c

```
1   #include <stdio.h>
2   #include <stdlib.h>
3   #include <libxml/parser.h>
4
5   int main()
6   {
7       const xmlChar *r = (const xmlChar *)"root";
8       xmlDocPtr doc;
9       xmlNodePtr root;
10
11      doc = xmlNewDoc( (const xmlChar *)"1.0");
12      root = xmlNewDocNode( doc, NULL, r, NULL);
13      xmlDocSetRootElement( doc, root );
14
15      xmlSaveFormatFile( "-", doc, 0 );
16
17      xmlFreeDoc(doc);
18
19      return(0);
20  }
```

Line 12 creates a new node, assigning its value to *xmlNodePtr* variable `root`. This variable is used in Line 13 to set the node as the document's root element. Line 15 outputs the result:

```
<?xml version="1.0"?>
<root/>
```

The XML data consists of two lines: the header and the root element. Because the root has no contents, it appears as an empty tag element.

Creating a child element

The function that creates a new element inside existing XML data is *xmlNewTextChild()*. As the name implies, the element created is a child node of an existing node. For XML data with only a root element, this function creates the first child, both giving it an element name and value.

The *xmlNewTextChild()* function has four arguments:

- An *xmlNodePtr* variable representing the parent node. The new element (child) is placed under this node

- An *xmlNsPtr* value representing the namespace for the new element, though `NULL` can be specified to inherit the parent's namespace

- The child element's name expressed as a *const xmlChar* string

- The child element's value expressed as a *const xmlChar* string

The value returned from *xmlNewTextChild()* is a pointer to the new node, or NULL if the operation failed.

The following code updates the preceding example 07-02_newxml2.c. A child element to the root is added with the results output.

07-03_newxml3.c

```
1   #include <stdio.h>
2   #include <stdlib.h>
3   #include <libxml/parser.h>
4
5   int main()
6   {
7       const xmlChar *r = (const xmlChar *)"root";
8       const xmlChar *element = (const xmlChar *)"data";
9       const xmlChar *value = (const xmlChar *)"Yes, I'm data!";
10      xmlDocPtr doc;
11      xmlNodePtr root,node;
12
13      doc = xmlNewDoc( (const xmlChar *)"1.0");
14      root = xmlNewDocNode( doc, NULL, r, NULL);
15      xmlDocSetRootElement( doc, root );
16      node = xmlNewTextChild( root, NULL, element, value);
17
18      xmlSaveFormatFile( "-", doc, 0 );
19
20      xmlFreeDoc(doc);
21
22      return(0);
23  }
```

Line 16 adds a new element and value to the root node. Variables element and value are declared at Lines 8 and 9.

In practice, the return value of node (at Line 16) should be tested against the NULL constant to ensure the function's success. When NULL is returned, the function fails.

Line 18 outputs the result:

```
<?xml version="1.0"?>
<root><data>Yes, I'm data!</data></root>
```

In the output, the root tag is expanded because it has content. The <data> tag is nested within the root. It's not formatted pretty because zero is specified (the final argument) in the *xmlSafeFormatFile()* function.

Sending the data to a new file

The examples so far in this Chapter have sent text to standard output. To save the created XML data to a file, only one change is need: the *xmlSaveFormatFile()* function must specify a filename, not the "-" abbreviation for standard output.

From source code file 07-03_newxml3.c the following change is made at Line 18:

07-04_newxml4.c

```
18    xmlSaveFormatFile( "new.xml", doc, 1 );
```

The first argument is a filename string. The third argument is 1, which formats the output in a pretty manner.

After running the program, you can view the new.xml file's contents, which are:

```
<?xml version="1.0"?>
<root>
  <data>Yes, I'm data!</data>
</root>
```

Adding encoding to the prolog

The second attribute appearing in an XML prolog, after the XML version number, is the data encoding. To add this tidbit to the XML prolog in a file you create, use the *xmlSaveFormatFileEnc()* function with a new argument: a string representing the encoding, such as "UTF-8".

The encoding argument appears as the third argument in the *xmlSaveFormatFileEnc()* function; the formatted output argument becomes the fourth argument when the encoding argument is present.

Here is the change made to Line 18 to add encoding to the output file:

07-05_newxml5.c

```
18    xmlSaveFormatFileEnc( "new.xml", doc, "UTF-8", 1 );
```

Above, the update to Line 18 for the source file 07-05_newxml5.c adds UTF-8 encoding to the output. It looks like this:

```
<?xml version="1.0" encoding="UTF-8"?>
<root>
  <data>Yes, I'm data!</data>
</root>
```

The encoding information, encoding="UTF-8", is set in the first line, the XML prolog.

The following source code shows a final, updated version of the newxml series of programs:

07-06_newxml6.c

```
1   #include <stdio.h>
2   #include <stdlib.h>
3   #include <libxml/parser.h>
4
5   int main()
6   {
7       const char filename[] = "new.xml";
8       const xmlChar *r = (const xmlChar *)"root";
9       const xmlChar *element = (const xmlChar *)"data";
10      const xmlChar *value = (const xmlChar *)"Yes, I'm data!";
11      xmlDocPtr doc;
12      xmlNodePtr root,node;
13      int x;
14
15      doc = xmlNewDoc( (const xmlChar *)"1.0");
16      root = xmlNewDocNode( doc, NULL, r, NULL);
17      xmlDocSetRootElement( doc, root );
18      node = xmlNewTextChild( root, NULL, element, value);
19
20      x = xmlSaveFormatFileEnc( filename, doc, "UTF-8", 1 );
21      if( x==-1 )
22          printf("Unable to create %s\n",filename);
23      else
24          printf("%s created, %d bytes written\n",filename,x);
25
26      xmlFreeDoc(doc);
27
28      return(0);
29  }
```

Sample output:

```
new.xml created, 84 bytes written
```

File dump for new.xml:

```
<?xml version="1.0" encoding="UTF-8"?>
<root>
  <data>Yes, I'm data!</data>
</root>
```

Adding a new element to any parent

The *xmlNewTextChild()* function not only builds new XML data in memory, it can add new elements to existing data. The process remains the same: Specify the parent element to which you want to add the child, then set the namespace (optional), element name, and its value.

The following code adds a new element <nemesis> to the sample.xml file. It's a new child of the root element, and it has the value "Underdog".

07-07_newnode.c

```
1   #include <stdio.h>
2   #include <stdlib.h>
3   #include <libxml/parser.h>
4
5   int main()
6   {
7       const char filename[] = "sample.xml";
8       xmlDocPtr doc;
9       xmlNodePtr root,newnode;
10      const xmlChar *element = (const xmlChar *)"nemesis";
11      const xmlChar *value = (const xmlChar *)"Underdog";
12
13      doc = xmlParseFile(filename);
14      if( doc==NULL )
15      {
16          fprintf(stderr,"Unable to process %s\n",filename);
17          exit(1);
18      }
19
20      root = xmlDocGetRootElement(doc);
21      newnode = xmlNewTextChild( root, NULL, element, value );
22      xmlSaveFormatFile( "-", doc, 1 );
23
24      xmlFreeDoc(doc);
25
26      return(0);
27  }
```

At Line 20, the *xmlDocGetRootElement()* function sets the top-level element in the XML data. This element is saved in the *xmlNodePtr* variable root. The element added will be a child of this node.

♦ *If you desire to create the new element as a child of another element, first browse to that element as demonstrated earlier in this book.*

At Line 21, the *xmlNewTextChild()* function creates a new child of the root node, uses *xmlChar* variables `element` and `value` as the new element's name and value, respectively.

Line 22 sends the XML data to standard output, which looks like this:

```
<?xml version="1.0" encoding="UTF-8"?>
<character>
        <firstName>Simon</firstName>
        <middleName>Bar</middleName>
        <lastName>Sinister</lastName>
        <address>
                <street>123 Evil Ave.</street>
                <city>Bigtown</city>
                <state>New York</state>
                <zip>12345</zip>
        </address>
        <isCartoon value="true"/>
        <IQ>213.5</IQ>
        <phone type="lab">212 555-1234</phone>
        <phone type="mobile">868 555-1234</phone>
        <assistant>Cad Lackey</assistant>
<nemesis>Underdog</nemesis></character>
```

The final line of output contains the new element, which is formatted in a lamentably awkward manner. Still, the addition is successful.

Saving data to a buffer

Saving XML data to a buffer in memory requires two functions:

• *xmlBufferCreate()*, which allocates an *xmlBufferPtr* variable

• *xmlNodeDump()*, which sends XML data to the *xmlBufferPtr* variable's storage

After these two functions have worked their magic, the XML data can be accessed from the *content* member of the *xmlBufferPtr* structure. This buffer contains plain text.

The *xmlBufferCreate()* function requires no arguments and returns an *xmlBufferPtr* variable. This variable is a pointer that references a structure containing details about the buffer created.

The *xmlNodeDump()* function processes the XML data and stores it in a buffer referenced by the *xmlBufferPtr* variable. This function has five arguments:

- An *xmlBufferPtr* variable, already created by using the *xmlBufferCreate()* function.

- The XML data's *xmlDocPtr* variable

- The *xmlNodePtr* variable for the top element to start dumping, typically the root element

- The imbrication level for indenting

- Formatting option

I'm uncertain about the effects of the last two arguments, but the first three are the most important. They dump the XML data into the buffer, automatically sized as required.

The *xmlNodeDump()* function returns the number of bytes sent to the buffer or -1 on error.

The following code updates source file 07-07_newnode.c to output the updated XML data saved in a buffer.

07-08_buffer.c

```
1   #include <stdio.h>
2   #include <stdlib.h>
3   #include <libxml/parser.h>
4
5   int main()
6   {
7       const char filename[] = "sample.xml";
8       xmlDocPtr doc;
9       xmlNodePtr root,newnode;
10      const xmlChar *element = (const xmlChar *)"nemesis";
11      const xmlChar *value = (const xmlChar *)"Underdog";
12      xmlBufferPtr buffer;
13
14      doc = xmlParseFile(filename);
15      if( doc==NULL )
16      {
17          fprintf(stderr,"Unable to process %s\n",filename);
18          exit(1);
19      }
20
21      root = xmlDocGetRootElement(doc);
22      newnode = xmlNewTextChild( root, NULL, element, value );
23
24      buffer = xmlBufferCreate();
25      xmlNodeDump(buffer,doc,root,4,1);
26      printf("%s\n",buffer->content);
27
28      xmlFreeDoc(doc);
29
30      return(0);
31  }
```

Line 12 declares *xmlBufferPtr* variable `buffer`. This variable is used at Line 24, storing the buffer created by the *xmlBufferCreate()* function.

Line 25 dumps the data into the buffer.

Line 26 outputs the buffer, displaying the updated XML data.

Here's the obligatory sample run output:

```
<character>
        <firstName>Simon</firstName>
        <middleName>Bar</middleName>
        <lastName>Sinister</lastName>
        <address>
                <street>123 Evil Ave.</street>
                <city>Bigtown</city>
                <state>New York</state>
                <zip>12345</zip>
        </address>
        <isCartoon value="true"/>
        <IQ>213.5</IQ>
        <phone type="lab">212 555-1234</phone>
        <phone type="mobile">868 555-1234</phone>
        <assistant>Cad Lackey</assistant>
<nemesis>Underdog</nemesis></character>
```

To instead output the data to a file, use the function *xmlSaveFormatFile()*, which is covered earlier in this Chapter.

8. The JSON Data Format

JSON stands for JavaScript Object Notation. This data exchange format has an advantage over XML in that it's more readable and better describes different data types. It's also rapidly becoming the most popular data storage format on the Internet.

Understanding JSON

Like XML, JSON data is presented as plain text. It follows a specific format and syntax, though the data itself is user-defined.

Key to the JSON format is the object, contained in braces or curly brackets. Within the object you find one more name/value pairs, such as:

```
{ "flavors":31 }
```

The name/value pair begins with the name enclosed in double quotes, a colon, and then a value: `"flavors"`:31.

The value can be a variety of data types, such as the integer value shown above, a string, double, Boolean, a list of objects, and so on.

A single object can contain multiple name value pairs, separated by commas:

```
{
  "name": "Dan",
  "age": 29,
  "weight": 179.4
}
```

The final name/value pair in the list lacks a trailing comma.

Other forms of data organization are possible as well, the details of which are covered in the later section, "Exploring JSON data types." At JSON's core, however, is the object containing one or more name/value pairs.

Obeying JSON syntax

The format for JSON data must balance. Objects must follow their format, double quotes matching, colons followed by data, commas used where necessary. Braces and brackets must match.

Whitespace in JSON data is optional. In fact, most JSON data generated on the Internet appears with little or no whitespace.

♦ *Whitespace includes spaces, linefeeds (\r), carriage returns (\n), and tabs (\t) which appear outside of a name/value pair.*

Exploring JSON data types

In a JSON name/value pair, the name can be whatever text is required to describe the data, enclosed in double quotes. After the colon appears one of several JSON data types:

STRING

Strings are enclosed in double quotes:

```
{
    "BookTtile": "DOS For Dummies"
}
```

As in C, a JSON string can include escaped characters, such as \n for the newline, \" for the double quote, and so on. Here's the full list:

\"	double quote
\\	backslash
\b	backspace
\f	form feed (clear screen)
\n	newline
\r	carriage return
\t	tab
\u*nnn*	hex value *nnnn*

NUMBER

Number values are expressed like numbers in C though, though without hexadecimal or octal notation:

```
{
    "Age": 969
```

```
}
```

Real numbers can also be expressed, which include a decimal in the value:

```
{
  "IQ": 135.9
}
```

E-notation values are also allowed:

```
{
  "Avogadro": 6.023e+23
}
```

♦ *Some numbers are stored as strings, not numbers. For example, a phone number or zip code is expressed as a string.*

OBJECT

Objects can be nested, one contained inside another:

```
{
  "Name":
    {
      "First": "Arthur",
      "Last": "Grockmeister"
    }
}
```

ORDERED LIST (ARRAY)

Ordered lists, also called arrays, are composed of multiple items of the same data type. A simple ordered list might be a set of integers:

```
{
  "HighScroes": [ 699, 522, 501, 427 ]
}
```

The array is enclosed in square brackets with each element separated by a comma. The final element lacks a comma.

An ordered list can include any valid JSON data type, including objects:

```
{
  "Books":
  [
    {
        "Title": "Home Surgery For Dummies",
        "Author": "Art Grockmeister"
    },
        "Title": "Yachting on Dry Land",
        "Author": "Willy Makit"
```

```
    },
      "Title": "Cats Make Terrible Pets",
      "Author": "Rufus Fido"
    }
  ]
}
```

Each object is separated by a comma and enclosed in square brackets, making the entire Books object an ordered list or array.

TRUE OR FALSE (BOOLEAN)

Boolean values are expressed as true or false:

```
{
  "YouAlive": true
}
```

And:

```
{
  "YouSkinny": false
}
```

NULL

The JSON null value represents no data. The name/value pair exists in the document, but the value is null or empty:

```
{
  "CommonSense": null
}
```

Studying the sample file

The file sample.json is used in the various sample files and is made available for this book. Here are its contents:

```
{
 "firstName": "Simon",
 "middleName": "Bar",
 "lastName": "Sinister",
 "address": {
   "street": "123 Evil Ave.",
   "city": "Bigtown",
   "state": "New York",
   "zip": "12345"
 },
 "isCartoon": true,
 "IQ": 213.5,
 "phones": [
   {
      "type": "lab",
```

```
      "number": "212 555-1234"
   },
   {
      "type": "mobile",
      "number": "868 555-1234"
   }
 ],
 "assistant": "Cad Lackey",
 "spouse": null,
 "favorite numbers": [ 2, 13, 23, 66 ]
}
```

This sample file contains a variety of the different objects found in JSON data: string, value, ordered list, Booleans, and null.

9. The json-c Library

The C language doesn't natively recognize the JSON data exchange format. To process the data, you can write your own code, but why bother? Instead, you can obtain, install, and use a third-party library.

Many third party JSON libraries are available to parse and create JSON data. The one I prefer and demonstrate in this book is json-c.

◆ *A major beef I have with the json-c library is that the function names are interminably long.*

Obtaining the json-c library

The json-c library has a home on GitHub:

`github.com/json-c/json-c`

You can install the library from this site, especially if you're using an IDE such as Code::Blocks.

If you prefer to code in a terminal window, especially to build the small examples shown in this book, I recommend you use the operating system's package manager to obtain and install the library, as described in the following section.

PACKAGE MANAGER INSTALLATION

If you're using a bash shell and the *apt* package manager, type this command to search for the json-c library:

```
sudo apt search libjson-c-dev
```

Type the superuser password, then peruse the list to look for the library, which should be the only search result. For example:

```
Sorting... Done
Full Text Search... Done
libjson-c-dev/bionic,now 0.12.1-1.3 amd64 [installed]
  JSON manipulation library - development files
```

The specific text you see varies, specifically the latter part of the third line. When you see the text [installed] appended, the library is already installed.

After confirming that the library is available, proceed with installation:

```
sudo apt-get libjson-c-dev
```

For the Macintosh, use Homebrew to obtain the json-c library:

```
brew search json-c
```

Refer to `brew.sh` for more details on Homebrew.

JSON-C LIBRARY API DOCUMENTATION

Even if you're using a package manager, a bonus of installing json-c from its GitHub site is that you can obtain the API documentation, which I recommend. To do so, obey these directions:

1. Create a directory in which you want to install the json-c files.

How you organize your file system is up to you. I created a `json-c` folder inside my main programming folder.

2. In the `json-c` folder, type:

```
git clone https://github.com/json-c/json-c.git
```

The library files are downloaded.

3. Look for the file named `Doxyfile`.

This file can be expanded to provide the API documentation, but only if you have the *doxygen* utility installed.

4. Confirm the presence of *doxygen*, type:

```
dpkg -s doxygen
```

On the Mac with Homebrew, type:

```
brew search doxygen
```

5. If you don't have *doxygen* installed, obtain it.

Type:

```
sudo apt-get install doxygen
```

On the Mac, type:

```
brew install doxygen
```

6. Once installed, ensure that you're in the same directory as the file named `Doxyfile`, and type:

```
doxygen
```

A doc directory tree is created.

7. Open the doc/html directory.

I recommend you perform this task in the GUI; open a folder window to view the html files.

8. Open the index.html file in your web browser to view the documentation.

Behold the API for the json-c library.

COPYING THE DOCUMENTATION IN WINDOWS 10

If you're using the Ubuntu shell in Windows 10, I recommend that you copy the html files – the API documentation – to a folder more accessible to Windows 10.

In Windows 10, I created a json-c documentation folder. To copy the html files to this folder, I typed the following command while in the html directory in the terminal window:

```
cp * /mnt/c/Users/Dan/Documents/json-c\ documentation/
```

My user profile folder in Windows 10 is c:\Users\Dan\, which appears in the command above. Otherwise, the files are copied to the folder \Documents\json-c documentation. From that location, I can access them locally in my web browser and study the API as I code.

Testing the json-c library installation

After installing the json-c library, the next step is to test the installation. You want to confirm that the header files and library are installed and configured. The following code assists in this task:

09-01_jsonctest.c

```
1  #include <stdio.h>
2  #include <json-c/json.h>
3
4  int main()
5  {
6         printf("json-c version %s\n",JSON_C_VERSION);
7
8         return(0);
9  }
```

The header file `json.h` is included at Line 2. It's located in the `json-c` directory. This directory is most likely installed in the `/uer/local/include` directory, though don't be surprised if it's found in `/usr/include`. If it's installed elsewhere and not symbolically linked to another location, compiling the code fails.

At Line 6, the current version of the json-c library is output, stored in the defined constant `JSON_C_VERSION`.

Compile and link with:

```
clang -ljson-c 02_06-jsontest1.c
```

First comes the compiler, *clang*, though you can use *gcc* or *cc* or whatever your favorite compiler might be. Then comes the command to link in the library, dash little-L and `json-c`. Finally comes the source code filename.

♦ *If you see linker errors, specify the linking option,* -ljson-c, *last.*

To run, type the default output filename, `./a.out`. Press Enter and the following output appears:

```
json-c version 0.12.1
```

You may see a more recent version, but the program works; the header file was found and the library properly linked in. You're ready to start using the json-c library to code in C.

10. JSON Data Access

Central to manipulating JSON data with the json-c library is creating a *json_object*. This is a variable, a pointer to a structure, that helps the library manage JSON data.

The *json_object* can be extracted from JSON data stored in a file or from a string representing JSON data within the source code. It can also be converted into a string for output and other manipulation.

Reading JSON data from a file

To JSON data stored in a file, use the *json_object_from_file()* function to open the file and read the data into a *json_object* variable. This function requires only one argument, a *const char* string representing the file to open:

```
jdata = json_object_from_file("sample.json");
```

Above, the file named `sample.json` is opened. Upon success, the *json_object* variable, the structure pointer `jdata` is filled with the necessary data. Upon failure, `NULL` is returned. Always test for the `NULL` condition when using *json_object_from_file()* to access a file.

10-01_jsonopen.c

```
1   #include <stdio.h>
2   #include <stdlib.h>
3   #include <json-c/json.h>
4
5   int main()
6   {
7       const char filename[] = "sample.json";
8       json_object *jdata;
9
10      jdata = json_object_from_file(filename);
11      if( jdata==NULL )
12      {
13          fprintf(stderr,"Unable to process %s\n",filename);
14          exit(1);
15      }
16      printf("File %s read successfully\n",filename);
17
18      return(0);
19  }
```

The *json_object* structure `jdata` is declared at Line 8. It must be a pointer, as shown in the code.

The *json_object_from_file()* function at Line 10 opens the file `sample.json` and fills `jdata` with the necessary info.

At Line 11, the NULL condition is tested. If true, the program exits with an appropriate error message. Otherwise a success message is output at Line 16.

Refer to the preceding chapter for compiling instructions.

Here's a sample run:

```
File sample.json read successfully
```

Outputting the JSON object

The *json_object_from_file()* function opens the file, reads in its contents, and parses the JSON data in preparation for conversion into a *json_object*. Internally, the *json_tokener_parse()* function is called to parse the data. This function is used directly on JSON string data; see the later section, "Processing a JSON string," for details on *json_tokener_parse()*.

Once opened and processed, *json_object* variable is ready for examination or manipulation. Various functions covered elsewhere in this book demonstrated how to cull through the data, pull out values, add new data, and modify the information.

To visually examine the data, and demonstrate that the JSON data was read, you can use the *json_object_to_json_string()* function. It translates a *json_object* into readable text: The function's sole argument is a *json_object* variable. The value returned is a *const char* pointer – a string representing the JSON data in a readable format.

In the following code, the string is output, showing the JSON data represented by the *json_object* processed from the `sample.json` file.

10-02_jsonoutupt.c

```
1  #include <stdio.h>
2  #include <stdlib.h>
3  #include <json-c/json.h>
4
5  int main()
```

```
6   {
7       const char filename[] = "sample.json";
8       json_object *jdata;
9       const char *jstring;
10
11      jdata = json_object_from_file(filename);
12      if( jdata==NULL )
13      {
14          fprintf(stderr,"Unable to process %s\n",filename);
15          exit(1);
16      }
17
18      jstring = json_object_to_json_string(jdata);
19      puts(jstring);
20
21      return(0);
22  }
```

This code is based on the preceding example, 10-01_jsonopen.c. The additions are at Line 9 with the declaration of the jstring pointer and Lines 18 and 19.

At Line 18, the *json_object* variable jdata is converted into a string, referenced by pointer jstring. Line 19 outputs the string, which looks like this:

```
{ "firstName": "Simon", "middleName": "Bar", "lastName":
"Sinister", "address": { "street": "123 Evil Ave.", "city":
"Bigtown", "state": "New York", "zip": "12345" },
"isCartoon": true, "IQ": 213.5, "phones": [ { "type":
"lab", "number": "212 555-1234" }, { "type": "mobile",
"number": "868 555-1234" } ], "assistant": "Cad Lackey",
"spouse": null, "favorite numbers": [ 2, 13, 23, 66 ] }
```

The output lacks fancy formatting. This is the way you find most JSON data in the wild. Further, this output isn't a mere echo of the file's text. Therefore, it demonstrates that the file's JSON data was parsed, stored in a *json_object*, and then processed back into text for output.

Outputting the JSON object with style

If you desire to output a JSON object in a more human-readable format, use the *json_object_to_json_string_ext()* function. It's related to the *json_object_to_json_string()* function, but with a second argument: a constant expressing how the string is to be formatted.

Several defined constants are available for use with the
json_object_to_json_string_ext() function. The one I use in the
following code is `JSON_C_TO_STRING_PRETTY`.

10-03_pretty.c

```
1   #include <stdio.h>
2   #include <stdlib.h>
3   #include <json-c/json.h>
4
5   int main()
6   {
7       const char filename[] = "sample.json";
8       json_object *jdata;
9       const char *jstring;
10
11      jdata = json_object_from_file(filename);
12      if( jdata==NULL )
13      {
14          fprintf(stderr,"Unable to process %s\n",filename);
15          exit(1);
16      }
17
18      jstring = json_object_to_json_string_ext(
19              jdata,
20              JSON_C_TO_STRING_PRETTY
21              );
22      puts(jstring);
23
24      return(0);
25  }
```

This code replaces Line 18 from the previous example code 10-
02_jsonoutput.c with the *json_object_to_json_string_ext()*
function. This function is split across four lines (to avoid
wrapping in this book). The output is far more readable:

```
{
  "firstName":"Simon",
  "middleName":"Bar",
  "lastName":"Sinister",
  "address":{
    "street":"123 Evil Ave.",
    "city":"Bigtown",
    "state":"New York",
    "zip":"12345"
  },
  "isCartoon":true,
  "IQ":213.5,
  "phones":[
    {
      "type":"lab",
      "number":"212 555-1234"
    },
    {
      "type":"mobile",
```

```
        "number":"868 555-1234"
      }
    ],
    "assistant":"Cad Lackey",
    "spouse":null,
    "favorite numbers":[
      2,
      13,
      23,
      66
    ]
}
```

The other constants you can use with the
json_object_to_json_string_ext() function are found in the API, on
the `json_object.h` reference page. Refer to Chapter 9 for details
on installing the API documentation.

Processing a JSON string

JSON data might not always be found in a file. For example,
your code may use the curl library to download JSON data from
a website, storing it in a buffer. If so, you can process that data
(string) into a JSON object for use with the json-c library.

To devour JSON data stored as a string, use the
json_tokener_parse() function. Its argument is a *const char* pointer
– a string – referencing JSON data. The value returned from the
function is a *json_object*.

After converting the string/text into a *json_object* variable, the
rest of your code works the same as if the *json_object* variable
was obtained from reading a file, as this code demonstrates:

10-04_string.c

```
1   #include <stdio.h>
2   #include <stdlib.h>
3   #include <json-c/json.h>
4
5   int main()
6   {
7       const char jstring[] = "{\"table\":\"B2\",\"guests\":4,\
8   \"orders\":[ \"Steak MR\",\"Halibut\",\
9   \"Fettuccine\",\"Lobster\"]}";
10      json_object *jdata;
11      const char *string;
12
13      jdata = json_tokener_parse(jstring);
14      if( jdata==NULL )
15      {
```

```
16          fprintf(stderr,"Unable to tokenize string\n");
17          exit(1);
18      }
19      string = json_object_to_json_string_ext(
20              jdata,
21              JSON_C_TO_STRING_PRETTY
22              );
23      puts(string);
24
25      return(0);
26  }
```

The JSON data string `jstring` appears starting at Line 7 and split between Lines 7, 8, and 9. The trailing backslash escapes the Enter key press at the end of the line; don't let the ugliness befuddle you.

At Line 19, the *json_object_to_json_string_ext()* function generates a string representing the *json_object*, which is redundant, I know, but the output is a lot prettier than the abbreviated, ugly string declared in the code. To wit:

```
{
  "table":"B2",
  "guests":4,
  "orders":[
    "Steak MR",
    "Halibut",
    "Fettuccine",
    "Lobster"
  ]
}
```

11. JSON Exploration

The process of culling through JSON data involves using the json-c library to transform the data (text) into a *json_object* variable. After doing so, the next step is to fetch the specific data chunk you need.

♦ *Remember, JSON data is user-defined. You must know what you're looking for within the data, a name or other object reference.*

Finding a JSON object

All JSON data is organized into objects containing one or more name/value pairs or one or more ordered lists. To obtain a tidbit of JSON data, you must know the name referencing a specific chunk of data.

When you know the name, use the *json_object_object_get_ex()* function to fetch details about the item. This function has three arguments:

• The *json_object* variable for the data you're plumbing, such as a value returned from the *json_object_from_file()* function

• A *constant char* value, a string representing the name in the name/value pair

• The address of a *json_object* pointer, which holds the result should the function find the named object

The value returned from the *json_object_object_get_ex()* function is true or false, depending on success. Unlike most json-c library functions, this one returns a Boolean indicating the function's success, with the value returned (a *json_object*) set as the third argument in the function.

11-01_objname.c

```
1  #include <stdio.h>
2  #include <stdlib.h>
3  #include <json-c/json.h>
4
5  int main()
6  {
7      const char filename[] = "sample.json";
8      const char object_name[] = "assistant";
```

```
 9      json_object *jdata,*objname;
10
11      jdata = json_object_from_file(filename);
12      if( jdata==NULL )
13      {
14          fprintf(stderr,"Unable to process %s\n",filename);
15          exit(1);
16      }
17
18      if( !json_object_object_get_ex(jdata,object_name,&objname))
19      {
20          fprintf(stderr,"Unable to find object '%s'\n",
21              object_name);
22          exit(1);
23      }
24      else
25      {
26          printf("Object '%s' found\n",object_name);
27      }
28
29      return(0);
30  }
```

This code searches the sample JSON data file, named at Line 7, looking for the key named `assistant`, as set on Line 8.

The data file is opened and converted into a *json_data* object `jdata` at Line 11.

Line 18 uses the *json_object_object_get_ex()* function to plumb the depths of `jdata` looking for the string represented by variable `object_name`. The result is saved in the `objname` variable, passed to the function as a pointer:

```
json_object_object_get_ex(jdata,object_name,&objname)
```

The value returned is true or false, which is negated at Line 18. In this manner, the *if* statement executes its statements when the function fails to locate the named object.

When the function returns true, a success message is output:

```
Object 'assistant' found
```

Obtaining the object's value is the next step. This operation is more complex than you may anticipate. It's covered in Chapter 12.

Walking peer-level entries

The json-c library can be of assistance when you don't know what objects dwell inside the JSON data. After obtaining a

json_object variable for the data, you have access to oodles of
information. One of the key functions used is
json_object_get_object():

```
entry = json_object_get_object(jdata);
```

The *json_object_get_object()* function accepts a *json_object* as an
argument and returns an *lh_table* structure pointer, such as `entry`
above. This variable represents a hash table of information about
the object. Specifically, members of the *lh_table* structure help
you reference objects within JSON data similar to the way a
linked list works.

For example, the *lh_table* structure member *head* points to the
first name/value pair in the JSON data list. The *lh_table* structure
member *tail* points to the last.

The items referenced by the *lh_table* structure member are
represented by another structure, *lh_entry*. It helps to think of
lh_table as a master list with the *lh_entry* structures referencing
each name/value pair individually.

The *lh_entry* structure has members *next* and *prev*, which you use
to access the new or previous name/value pairs in the chain.
Further, *lh_entry* structure members *k* and *v* represent keys
(names) and values for each name/value pair, as the following
code demonstrates:

11-02_entrylist.c

```
1   #include <stdio.h>
2   #include <stdlib.h>
3   #include <json-c/json.h>
4
5   int main()
6   {
7       const char filename[] = "sample.json";
8       json_object *jdata;
9       struct lh_entry *entry;
10      char *key;
11
12      jdata = json_object_from_file(filename);
13      if( jdata==NULL )
14      {
15          fprintf(stderr,"Unable to process %s\n",filename);
16          exit(1);
17      }
18
19      entry = json_object_get_object(jdata)->head;
20      while( entry )
21      {
22          key = (char *)entry->k;
```

```
23          printf("Object '%s' found\n",key);
24          entry = entry->next;
25      }
26
27      return(0);
28  }
```

At Line 19, the *json_object_get_object()* function is used on the `jdata` variable, which was read and parsed from file `sample.json` at Line 12. The *head* member of the structure, the first peer-level item in the list, is returned and stored in *lh_entry* variable `entry` at Line 19.

The *while* loop at Line 20 walks through each item in the table, just like a linked list: The string `key` is obtained from the entry's *k* member, then output at Line 23. The next object in the list is linked to at Line 24.

The output shows the top-level objects in the file:

```
Object 'firstName' found
Object 'middleName' found
Object 'lastName' found
Object 'address' found
Object 'isCartoon' found
Object 'IQ' found
Object 'phones' found
Object 'assistant' found
Object 'spouse' found
Object 'favorite numbers' found
```

The list represents only the top level of data in the file.

JSON objects can also be nested, which is the case for object `address` in the `sample.json` file (output above). To explore the next level requires a bit more magic, which is covered in the later section, "Recursively extracting data types."

12. JSON Data Extraction

Once you locate a JSON object by name, the next step is to read its data – the value part of the name/value pair. (The json-c library uses the terms key/value.)

Before you can access the data, however, you must determine the object's data type. This step is necessary because json-c uses different functions to read different data types. After you know the data type, your code can set which function is used to ultimately obtain the data stored in a name/value pair or JSON object.

Recognizing JSON data types

The *json_object_get_type()* function obtains the data type for a *json_object* value. This function has one argument, a *json_object* variable. The value returned is an enumerated integer *json_type*. This variable can be declared as follows:

```
enum json_type type;
```

The variable declared, `type` (for example), is then compared with constants representing the JSON object data types:

json_type_array
json_type_boolean
json_type_double
json_type_int
json_type_null
json_type_object
json_type_string

This enumeration is documented in the json-c library API html files, see the `json_object.h` documentation.

A positive comparison is how you can match up the type of data associated the name of a JSON name/value pair. For example, the type of data associated with an object named `high_score` might be an integer, or *json_type_int*.

Typically, a *switch-case* structure is used to determine, read, or modify the value's data. The following code demonstrates how the different data types are identified.

12-01_types.c

```
 1   #include <stdio.h>
 2   #include <stdlib.h>
 3   #include <json-c/json.h>
 4
 5   int main()
 6   {
 7       const char filename[] = "sample.json";
 8       const char object_name[] = "assistant";
 9       json_object *jdata,*objname;
10       enum json_type type;
11
12       jdata = json_object_from_file(filename);
13       if( jdata==NULL )
14       {
15           fprintf(stderr,"Unable to process %s\n",filename);
16           exit(1);
17       }
18
19       if( !json_object_object_get_ex(jdata,object_name,&objname))
20       {
21           fprintf(stderr,"Unable to find object %s\n",
22               object_name);
23           exit(1);
24       }
25
26       printf("The object type of '%s' is ",object_name);
27       type = json_object_get_type(objname);
28       switch(type)
29       {
30           case json_type_array:
31               puts("array");
32               break;
33           case json_type_boolean:
34               puts("boolean");
35               break;
36           case json_type_double:
37               puts("double");
38               break;
39           case json_type_int:
40               puts("integer");
41               break;
42           case json_type_null:
43               puts("null");
44               break;
45           case json_type_object:
46               puts("object");
47               break;
48           case json_type_string:
49               puts("string");
50               break;
51           default:
52               puts("unrecognized");
53       }
54
55       return(0);
56   }
```

This first part of this code is based on the earlier example `11-01_objname`. At Line 27, new code starts with the *json_object_get_type()* function. The argument is the `objname` *json_object* variable and the value returned is enumerated *json_type* variable `type`.

After the data type is obtained, the *switch-case* structure starting at Line 28 compares the `type` variable with all the *json_type* constants to output the data type found:

```
The object type of 'assistant' is string
```

After determining the data type, the proper function can be used to pull the value associated with the name. Details on this operation are covered starting in the later section, "Extracting an object's value."

Getting all the data types

To obtain values associated with objects, you "walk through" the various object within JSON data. Unlike the example from Chapter 11, however, you use the *lh_entry* structure to read both the object's name (key) and value. The structure is also used to walk through objects in the data.

Yeah, that's a lot of detail. I'll break it down.

First, after obtaining the *json_object* for JSON data in a file, use the *json_object_get_object()* function to return the object, but immediately grab the *head* member of the structure:

```
entry = json_object_get_object(jdata)->head;
```

This technique was demonstrated in Chapter 11: The *json_object*'s *head* member refers to the first item in a list of name/value pairs. This statement returns an *lh_entry* structure pointer, variable `entry` above. As stated in the earlier section, "Walking the entries," an *lh_entry* structure pointer works like a linked list. Some of its notable members of this structure include:

lh_entry->k, a string representing the key or object name

lh_entry->v, a pointer referencing the object's value

lh_entry->next, the next peer-level object in the list

lh_entry->prev, the previous peer-level object in the list

To obtain the object value's data type, use the
json_object_get_type() function on the *lh_entry->v* member. For
example:

```
val = (struct json_object *)entry->v;
type = json_object_get_type(val);
```

Above, val is the *lh_entry->v* value – the object's value – and
type is an *enum json_type* variable, representing one of the
several JSON object data types. You can then use a *switch-case*
structure to deal with the different JSON data types, as shown in
this code:

12-02_objects.c

```
1    #include <stdio.h>
2    #include <stdlib.h>
3    #include <json-c/json.h>
4
5    int main()
6    {
7        const char filename[] = "sample.json";
8        json_object *jdata;
9        enum json_type type;
10       struct lh_entry *entry;
11       char *key;
12       struct json_object *val;
13
14       jdata = json_object_from_file(filename);
15       if( jdata==NULL )
16       {
17           fprintf(stderr,"Unable to process %s\n",filename);
18           exit(1);
19       }
20
21       entry = json_object_get_object(jdata)->head;
22       while( entry )
23       {
24           key = (char *)entry->k;
25           val = (struct json_object *)entry->v;
26           printf("'%s' type is ",key);
27           type = json_object_get_type(val);
28           switch(type)
29           {
30               case json_type_array:
31                   puts("array");
32                   break;
33               case json_type_boolean:
34                   puts("boolean");
35                   break;
36               case json_type_double:
37                   puts("double");
38                   break;
39               case json_type_int:
40                   puts("integer");
41                   break;
```

```
42          case json_type_null:
43              puts("null");
44              break;
45          case json_type_object:
46              puts("object");
47              break;
48          case json_type_string:
49              puts("string");
50              break;
51          default:
52              puts("unrecognized");
53          }
54      entry = entry->next;
55      }
56
57      return(0);
58 }
```

Line 21 obtains the *lh_entry* pointer variable `entry` from the *json_ojbect_get_object()* function. Variable `entry` references the first object in the JSON data referenced by `jdata`.

The *while* loop at Line 22 processes each peer-level object in the list. Variables `key` and `val` are assigned at Lines 24 and 25. The `key` string is output at Line 26.

Line 27 obtains the data type referenced by variable `val`. A *switch-case* structure outputs the object's data type:

```
'firstName' type is string
'middleName' type is string
'lastName' type is string
'address' type is object
'isCartoon' type is boolean
'IQ' type is double
'phones' type is array
'assistant' type is string
'spouse' type is null
'favorite numbers' type is array
```

This output reflects only the top-level objects. It doesn't explore nested objects, where the value is an object. (Item `address` above is an example of a nested object.) Nor does this code explore any arrays.

Remember: Knowing an object's data type is important because a specific library function is required to extract a key's value based on its data type.

Extracting an object's value

After obtaining the data type for a name/value pair, your code can use a specific json-c library function to obtain the value's data; each data type has its own extraction function.

For example, if the data type returned is a string, the *json_object_get_string()* function is used to fetch the string. This function accepts a *json_object* variable as an argument – the name/value pair – and returns a *const char* pointer – the string value.

Before fetching the value, you must locate the data. As shown in Chapter 11, the *json_object_object_get_ex()* function obtains a *json_object* variable for a specific name in the name/value pair:

```
json_object_object_get_ex(jdata,name,&object);
```

Above, `jdata` would be the parent *json_object*. The function locates an object matching the variable `name` and places that object's data in the *json_object* variable `object`.

Once you have the named *json_object*, you use the appropriate function to extract its value, such as *json_object_get_string()*:

```
value = json_object_get_string(object);
```

Above, `object` is a *json_object* returned from the *json_object_object_get_ex()* function. Variable `value` holds the *char* pointer returned, the string matching the named object. Once the string's value is extracted, it can be output like any string.

12-03_value.c

```
1   #include <stdio.h>
2   #include <stdlib.h>
3   #include <json-c/json.h>
4
5   int main()
6   {
7       const char filename[] = "sample.json";
8       const char name[] = "assistant";
9       const char *value;
10      json_object *jdata,*object;
11
12      jdata = json_object_from_file(filename);
13      if( jdata==NULL )
14      {
15          fprintf(stderr,"Unable to process %s\n",filename);
16          exit(1);
17      }
```

```
18
19          json_object_object_get_ex(jdata,name,&object);
20          value = json_object_get_string(object);
21          printf("'%s''s value is %s\n'",name,value);
22
23          return(0);
24    }
```

Line 19 obtains the object matching the `name` variable, declared at Line 8. The object is returned in *json_object* variable `object`, the function's third argument (Line 19).

♦ *In your code, you must test the return condition of the json_object_object_get_ex() function (Line 19), true or false. If false, the named object isn't found.*

The `object` variable is used at Line 19 with the function *json_object_get_string()* to return the string's address in variable `value`, which is then output at Line 21:

```
'assistant''s value is Cad Lackey
```

This code works to find the string value of a top-level object in the JSON data. Nested objects must be searched recursively, as covered in the later section, "Recursively extracting data types."

Extracting different data types

For each JSON data type, a different function is used to fetch the value in a name/value pair. Here are four functions for four JSON data types:

json_object_get_boolean()
json_object_get_double()
json_object_get_int()
json_object_get_string()

A function to fetch the null data type isn't necessary; once your code identifies a null object, that's it. (See Line 51 in the sample code below, `12-04_datatypes.c`.)

The other two data types, array and object, require special attention covered in the later sections "Reading data from an array" and "Recursively extracting data types," respectively.

The following code churns through the top-level objects in the JSON data file `sample.json`. For the four data types – Boolean, double, int, and string – the name/value pair's data is output. The null data type is also identified.

12-04_datatypes.c

```
1   #include <stdio.h>
2   #include <stdlib.h>
3   #include <json-c/json.h>
4
5   int main()
6   {
7       const char filename[] = "sample.json";
8       json_object *jdata,*object;
9       enum json_type type;
10      struct lh_entry *entry;
11      char *key;
12      const char *jstring;
13      int jint,jbool;
14      double jdouble;
15      struct json_object *val;
16
17      jdata = json_object_from_file(filename);
18      if( jdata==NULL )
19      {
20          fprintf(stderr,"Unable to process %s\n",filename);
21          exit(1);
22      }
23
24      entry=json_object_get_object(jdata)->head;
25      while(entry)
26      {
27          key = (char *)entry->k;
28          val = (struct json_object *)entry->v;
29          json_object_object_get_ex(jdata, key, &object);
30          printf("'%s' type is ",key);
31          type = json_object_get_type(val);
32          switch(type)
33          {
34              case json_type_array:
35                  puts("an array");
36                  break;
37              case json_type_boolean:
38                  jbool = json_object_get_boolean(object);
39                  printf("boolean, value: %s\n",
40                          (jbool?"TRUE":"FALSE")
41                      );
42                  break;
43              case json_type_double:
44                  jdouble = json_object_get_double(object);
45                  printf("double, value: %f\n", jdouble);
46                  break;
47              case json_type_int:
48                  jint = json_object_get_int(object);
49                  printf("integer, value: %d\n",jint);
50                  break;
51              case json_type_null:
52                  printf("null, value: NULL\n");
53                  break;
```

```
54              case json_type_object:
55                  puts("an object");
56                  break;
57              case json_type_string:
58                  jstring = json_object_get_string(object);
59                  printf("string, value: %s\n",jstring);
60                  break;
61              default:
62                  puts("Unrecognized");
63          }
64          entry=entry->next;
65      }
66
67      return(0);
68  }
```

The *while* loop processes all top-level objects in the JSON data in the `sample.json` file. For each item, the name and value are obtained (Lines 27 and 28) and a *json_object* `object` is fetched for the named `key` at Line 29. The value's data type, variable `type`, is returned at Line 31.

The *switch-case* structure examines the object's data type at Line 32. Various *case* statements match the data types, with values obtained for Boolean, double, integer, and string objects:

Line 37 handles Boolean data. The *json_object_get_boolean()* function returns the value. The *printf()* statement, split between Lines 39 to 41, uses the ternary operator to output TRUE or FALSE.

Line 43 handles double data types, using *json_object_get_double()* to return the *double* value into variable `jdouble`. Line 45 outputs the value.

Line 47 handles integer data by using the *json_object_get_int()* function.

Line 51 handles the null data type. No further processing is necessary.

Finally, at Line 57, strings are processed as covered earlier in this Chapter.

Here is sample output:

```
'firstName' type is string, value: Simon
'middleName' type is string, value: Bar
'lastName' type is string, value: Sinister
'address' type is an object
'isCartoon' type is boolean, value: TRUE
'IQ' type is double, value: 213.500000
'phones' type is an array
'assistant' type is string, value: Cad Lackey
```

```
'spouse' type is null, value: NULL
'favorite numbers' type is an array
```

Reading data from an array

When a JSON object's value is identified as an array, your code has a few hoops to jump through (and at least one loop) to process the array's elements. The order of operations works like this:

1. Obtain the array's length.
2. Fetch a *json_object* for a specific element in the array.
3. Determine the *json_object*'s data type.
4. Use the appropriate function to fetch the data type's value.
5. Repeat Steps 2 through 4 for each element in the array.

Of course, if you just need one element and you know the element's data type, you can skip some steps. Otherwise, the breakdown of events, along with the necessary functions, looks like this:

The *json_object_array_length()* function returns the number of elements in the array as an integer value. Its argument is the *json_object* variable representing the array:

```
elements = json_object_array_length(keyname);
```

Above, `keyname` is the *json_object* variable for the array. The value returned is stored in *int* variable `elements`.

To obtain an array element, the function *json_object_array_get_idx()* is used. Its two arguments are the *json_object* variable representing the array and an integer value representing the array element number to fetch. As with arrays in C, the first element is zero:

```
jelement = json_object_array_get_idx(keyname,x);
```

Above, `keyname` is the array *json_object* and `x` is an *int* variable representing the element number. The value returned, `jelement`, is yet another *json_object*. You use this value with the proper function to fetch the array element's value based on its data type. For example, if the array is composed of integers, you use the *json_object_get_int()* function on the `jelement` variable.

12-05_arrays.c

```
1   #include <stdio.h>
```

```
 2   #include <stdlib.h>
 3   #include <json-c/json.h>
 4
 5   int main()
 6   {
 7       const char filename[] = "sample.json";
 8       json_object *jdata,*keyname,*jelement;
 9       enum json_type type;
10       struct lh_entry *entry;
11       char *key;
12       const char *jstring;
13       int jint,jbool,elements,x;
14       double jdouble;
15       struct json_object *val;
16
17       jdata = json_object_from_file(filename);
18       if( jdata==NULL )
19       {
20           fprintf(stderr,"Unable to process %s\n",filename);
21           exit(1);
22       }
23
24       entry=json_object_get_object(jdata)->head;
25       while(entry)
26       {
27           key = (char *)entry->k;
28           val = (struct json_object *)entry->v;
29           json_object_get_ex(jdata, key, &keyname);
30           printf("'%s' type is ",key);
31           type = json_object_get_type(val);
32           switch(type)
33           {
34               case json_type_array:
35                   elements = json_object_array_length(keyname);
36                   printf("an array with %d elements:",elements);
37                   for( x=0; x<elements; x++)
38                   {
39                       jelement=json_object_array_get_idx(
40                               keyname,
41                               x
42                               );
43                       printf(" %d",json_object_get_int(jelement));
44                   }
45                   putchar('\n');
46                   break;
47               case json_type_boolean:
48                   jbool = json_object_get_boolean(keyname);
49                   printf("boolean, value: %s\n",
50                           (jbool?"TRUE":"FALSE")
51                           );
52                   break;
53               case json_type_double:
54                   jdouble = json_object_get_double(keyname);
55                   printf("double, value: %f\n", jdouble);
56                   break;
57               case json_type_int:
58                   jint = json_object_get_int(keyname);
59                   printf("integer, value: %d\n",jint);
```

```
60              break;
61          case json_type_null:
62              printf("null, value: NULL\n");
63              break;
64          case json_type_object:
65              puts("an object");
66              break;
67          case json_type_string:
68              jstring = json_object_get_string(keyname);
69              printf("string, value: %s\n",jstring);
70              break;
71          default:
72              puts("Unrecognized");
73          }
74          entry=entry->next;
75      }
76
77      return(0);
78  }
```

Don't let this sample code's length intimidate you! It's effectively the same as the previous example, `12-04_datatypes.c`, with the `case json_type_array:` section fleshed out – plus the addition of a few variables.

In the `case json_type_array:` section, the number of array elements is obtained at Line 35 and stored in variable `elements`. This value is output at Line 36.

At Line 37, a *for* loop processes all the elements; the first element number is zero, just like any C language array.

The statement at Line 39 is split between four lines. It fetches a *json_object* `jelement` for each element in the array. Line 43 uses the *json-object_get_int()* function to output the integer's value.

As is always the case, this code knows the array's data type ahead of time; the array contains integers. Regardless, you must always use the correct function to extract the values.

Here's sample output, with the array appearing as the last line:

```
'firstName' type is string, value: Simon
'middleName' type is string, value: Bar
'lastName' type is string, value: Sinister
'address' type is an object
'isCartoon' type is boolean, value: TRUE
'IQ' type is double, value: 213.500000
'phones' type is an array with 2 elements: 0 0
'assistant' type is string, value: Cad Lackey
'spouse' type is null, value: NULL
'favorite numbers' type is an array with 4 elements: 2 13
23 66
```

Recursively extracting data types

The only data type not yet covered in this Chapter is the nested object. Extracting this data type begs for a recursive function. After all, the nested object can contain any other data type – including another nested object.

To craft a recursive function, I built upon the source code file 12-05_array.c from the preceding section, removing the key part of the code to create a function *parse_json_object()*.

The *parse_json_object()* function requires three arguments:

- A *json_object* to parse, which can be the top-level object or any JSON data that has an object as its data type.

- The *lh_entry* structure representing the start of the objects to process – like the head of a linked list.

- An indent value, which prettifies the output.

This function is called initially to process the JSON data. It's called again when a name/value pair is identified as an object:

12-06_recursive.c

```
1    #include <stdio.h>
2    #include <stdlib.h>
3    #include <json-c/json.h>
4
5    void parse_json_object(
6            json_object *jobj,
7            struct lh_entry *ent,
8            int indent)
9    {
10       json_object *keyname,*jelement;
11       enum json_type type;
12       char *key;
13       const char *jstring;
14       int jint,jbool,elements,x;
15       struct json_object *val;
16       struct lh_entry *e;
17
18       while(ent)
19       {
20           key = (char *)ent->k;
21           val = (struct json_object *)ent->v;
22           json_object_object_get_ex(jobj, key, &keyname);
23           printf("%*c'%s' type is ",indent*4,' ',key);
24           type = json_object_get_type(val);
25           switch(type)
26           {
27               case json_type_array:
```

```
28                    elements = json_object_array_length(keyname);
29                    printf("array with %d elements:",elements);
30                    for( x=0; x<elements; x++)
31                    {
32                        jelement=json_object_array_get_idx(
33                            keyname,
34                            x
35                            );
36                        printf(" %d",json_object_get_int(jelement));
37                    }
38                    putchar('\n');
39                    break;
40                case json_type_boolean:
41                    jbool = json_object_get_boolean(keyname);
42                    printf("boolean, value: %s\n",
43                            (jbool?"TRUE":"FALSE")
44                        );
45                    break;
46                case json_type_double:
47                    puts("Double");
48                    break;
49                case json_type_int:
50                    jint = json_object_get_int(keyname);
51                    printf("integer, value: %d\n",jint);
52                    break;
53                case json_type_null:
54                    puts("Null");
55                    break;
56                case json_type_object:
57                    puts("JSON object:");
58                    e = json_object_get_object(keyname)->head;
59                    parse_json_object(keyname,e,indent+1);
60                    break;
61                case json_type_string:
62                    jstring = json_object_get_string(keyname);
63                    printf("string, value: %s\n",jstring);
64                    break;
65                default:
66                    puts("Unrecognized");
67            }
68        ent=ent->next;
69        }
70 }
71
72 int main()
73 {
74     const char filename[] = "sample.json";
75     json_object *jdata;
76     struct lh_entry *entry;
77
78     jdata = json_object_from_file(filename);
79     if( jdata==NULL )
80     {
81         fprintf(stderr,"Unable to process %s\n",filename);
82         exit(1);
83     }
84
85     entry=json_object_get_object(jdata)->head;
```

```
86        parse_json_object(jdata,entry,0);
87
88        return(0);
89   }
```

The code's length may frighten you, but it's built upon the previous two examples, with the *while* loop part of the code thrust into its own function, *parse_json_object()*. This function starts at Line 5. I split the declaration across several lines to avoid ugly text-wrapping issues in this book.

The *main()* function at Line 72, opens the sample file and obtains the first *json_object* variable, `jdata`. The *head* member of the object's *lh_entry* structure is obtained, then passed to the *parse_json_object()* function at Line 86.

Within the *parse_json_object()* function, a *while* loop (Line 18) processes each peer-level object, obtaining its name and value type. Each type is processed in the *switch-case* structure at Line 25.

When an object data type is processed, it has a value of *json_type_object*. Line 56 obtains the object's *lh_entry head* member and recursively calls the *parse_json_object()* function to repeat the process. This is how the values for the `sample.json` file's `address` object are output:

```
'firstName' type is string, value: Simon
'middleName' type is string, value: Bar
'lastName' type is string, value: Sinister
'address' type is JSON object:
   'street' type is string, value: 123 Evil Ave.
   'city' type is string, value: Bigtown
   'state' type is string, value: New York
   'zip' type is string, value: 12345
'isCartoon' type is boolean, value: TRUE
'IQ' type is Double
'phones' type is array with 2 elements: 0 0
'assistant' type is string, value: Cad Lackey
'spouse' type is Null
'favorite numbers' type is array with 4 elements: 2 13 23
66
```

The `indent` argument for *prase_json_object()* indents the child objects, as shown in the output.

Also visible in the output is the code's inability to process the `phones` array. This is due to the *case* statements for *json_type_array* (Line 27), which assume the array contains only integer values, not objects. To handle object, you must add more code to evaluate the type of array element and then process it accordingly. I'll leave this exercise for you to complete, though be aware that when it comes to JSON data, you know what types are available and what to test for.

13. JSON Output

Using the json-c library, you can write C code that pops JSON data instantly into existence. The key is to create a *json_object* variable and then pack it full of JSON objects, name/value pairs. You can then write the main *json_object* variable's JSON data out to a file or convert it into a string for whatever.

Building JSON data from scratch

As with reading JSON data in the json-c library, creating JSON data involves making a new *json_object* variable. Once created, the object is assigned JSON data in the form of a new object. The new object's data is created first, then it's assigned a name and associated with the main or top *json_object* variable, like a child to a parent.

THE NEW JSON_OBJECT

To create a new *json_object*, into which you can pack JSON data, use the *json_object_new_object()* function. It has no arguments and returns a *json_object* value. If the function fails, NULL is returned, otherwise the *json_object* value returned can be used to store data in the form of JSON objects.

The following code demonstrates how *json_object_new_object()* works, using the *json_object_to_json_string_ext()* function to output the results.

13-01_newobject.c

```
1   #include <stdio.h>
2   #include <stdlib.h>
3   #include <json-c/json.h>
4
5   int main()
6   {
7       json_object *newobj;
8       const char *jstring;
9
10      newobj = json_object_new_object();
11      if( newobj==NULL )
12      {
13          fprintf(stderr,"Unable to create object\n");
14          exit(1);
15      }
```

```
16        puts("New object created:");
17        jstring = json_object_to_json_string_ext(
18               newobj,
19               JSON_C_TO_STRING_PRETTY
20               );
21        puts(jstring);
22
23        return(0);
24    }
```

The two arguments to *json_object_to_json_string_ext()* are the
json_object variable, newobj, and the constant
JSON_C_TO_STRING_PRETTY, which prettifies the output:

```
New object created:
{
}
```

The object contains no data; it's empty. Yet it's prepared to host
some name/value pairs, which are created in the next step.

NEW JSON DATA

The process of creating new JSON data – a new name/value pair
– works like this:

1. Create a *json_object* in which to store the name/value pair.
2. Create the new value by data type, a string, integer, and so on.
3. Add the new data type to the *json_object* created in Step 1,
   assigning it a name.
4. Repeat Steps 2 and 3 as needed.

The first step is covered in the preceding section. The second
step involves using a specific function for the JSON data type
you want to create. For example, to add a string object, you use
the *json_object_new_string()* function. This function creates the
value (data) as a *json_object* variable.

The third step is handled by the *json_object_object_add()* function.
This function requires three arguments:

- The *json_object* variable with which to associate the new
  name/value pair, the main or parent-level object

- A *const char* pointer representing a string for the object's
  name

- The *json_object* variable returned from the function that
  created the data, such as *json_object_new_string()*, or similar
  functions for different types of JSON data

Finally, you repeat Steps 2 and 3 as needed to build the JSON data.

To summarize, you need two *json_object* variables to complete this operation: one as an outer container and another as a container for the new name/value pair. The value is supplied as a *json_object* generated by a function specific to the value type, and the name is assigned when the name/value pair created by using the *json_object_object_add()* function.

Here's sample code to illustrate:

13-02_jsondata.c

```
1   #include <stdio.h>
2   #include <stdlib.h>
3   #include <json-c/json.h>
4
5   int main()
6   {
7       json_object *newobj,*newdata;
8       const char value[] = "Arthur Grockmeister";
9       const char name[] = "username";
10      const char *jstring;
11
12      newobj = json_object_new_object();
13      if( newobj==NULL )
14      {
15          fprintf(stderr,"Unable to create object\n");
16          exit(1);
17      }
18      puts("New object created:");
19
20      newdata = json_object_new_string(value);
21      if( newdata==NULL )
22      {
23          fprintf(stderr,"Unable to create string object\n");
24          exit(1);
25      }
26
27      json_object_object_add( newobj, name, newdata );
28      jstring = json_object_to_json_string_ext(
29              newobj,
30              JSON_C_TO_STRING_PRETTY
31              );
32      puts(jstring);
33
34      return(0);
35  }
```

The main *json_object* `newobj` is created at Line 12. Line 20 creates another *json_object*, `newdata`, which is a new string. This string is merely data; it doesn't have a name associated with it.

At Line 27, the items created are married: the string data in newdata is assigned the value of the string variable name. This new object is associated with newobj to form JSON data with a single, string object.

Line 28 converts the object to a string, stored in variable jstring, which is output at Line 32:

```
New object created:
{
  "username":"Arthur Grockmeister"
}
```

OTHER JSON DATA TYPES

As you might guess, different json-c library functions are used to create new data types. Here's the full list:

json_object_new_array()
json_object_new_boolean()
json_object_new_double()
json_object_new_int()
json_object_new_object()
json_object_new_string()

A specific command isn't available to create a null object. Because the object is null, use the *json_object_object_add()* function to create it as follows:

```
json_object_object_add(newobj, obj_name, NULL);
```

Above, the first argument newobj is the main *json_object*, the outer container; the second argument obj_name is a *const char* string defining the null object's name; the final argument is the NULL constant. This statement creates a name/value pair with *null* as the value.

The preceding section covers creating a string object. The functions for creating Boolean, double, and integer objects are straightforward, as covered in this section. Later sections explore creating array objects and nested objects.

The function *json_object_new_boolean()* has a single argument, a *json_bool* variable either 1 or 0:

```
newdata = json_object_new_boolean( (json_bool)0 );
```

The sole argument for the *json_object_new_double()* function is a *double* value, variable, constant, or expression:

```
newdata = json_object_new_double(33.0/55.1);
```

For an integer object, the argument for *json_object_new_int()* is an integer value:

```
newdata = json_object_new_int(age);
```

Each of these three functions returns a *json_object* variable, holding the address of a structure containing the data created. If the functions fail, the variable is NULL. Always test for this condition in your code; in the following example, I omit testing for brevity's sake.

13-03_moredata.c

```
1   #include <stdio.h>
2   #include <stdlib.h>
3   #include <json-c/json.h>
4
5   int main()
6   {
7       json_object *newobj,*newdata;
8       const char b_name[] = "isReal";
9       const char d_name[] = "iq";
10      const char i_name[] = "age";
11      const char n_name[] = "smell";
12      const char s_value[] = "Arthur Grockmeister";
13      const char s_name[] = "username";
14      const char *jstring;
15
16      newobj = json_object_new_object();
17      if( newobj==NULL )
18      {
19          fprintf(stderr,"Unable to create object\n");
20          exit(1);
21      }
22      puts("New object created:");
23
24      /* bool */
25      newdata = json_object_new_boolean( (json_bool)0 );
26      json_object_object_add(newobj,b_name,newdata);
27      /* double */
28      newdata = json_object_new_double(212.0);
29      json_object_object_add(newobj,d_name,newdata);
30      /* int */
31      newdata = json_object_new_int(59);
32      json_object_object_add(newobj,i_name,newdata);
33      /* null */
34      json_object_object_add(newobj,n_name,NULL);
35      /* string */
36      newdata = json_object_new_string(s_value);
37      json_object_object_add(newobj,s_name,newdata );
38
39      jstring = json_object_to_json_string_ext(
40              newobj,
41              JSON_C_TO_STRING_PRETTY
```

```
42              );
43      puts(jstring);
44
45      return(0);
46  }
```

Lines 24 through 27 creates name/value pairs – objects – for the newobj *json_object* created at Line 16.

You may have observed that I re-use the *json_object* variable newdata for each of the new name/value pairs created (Lines 25, 28, 31, and 36). This approach is okay because the object is created and assigned; after using the *json_object_object_add()* function (Lines 26, 29, 32, and 37) you can re-use the newdata *json_object* variable.

The program's output lists the five objects created and added to the JSON data:

```
New object created:
{
  "isReal":false,
  "iq":212,
  "age":59,
  "smell":null,
  "username":"Arthur Grockmeister"
}
```

The objects appear in the list in the order they were added, as shown in the code.

Building an array object (ordered list)

To create an array or ordered list object, your code must go through three steps:

1. Create a new array object.
2. Create and add elements.
3. Add the array object to a parent JSON object.

First, the *json_object_new_array()* function creates a new array object. The function requires no arguments and returns a *json_object* pointer variable, NULL upon failure.

The array is created as an empty object. The second step is to add elements, each of which is some type of JSON data, such as an integer, string, or what-have-you. The same functions listed in the earlier section, "Other JSON data types," are used to create these values.

Use the *json_object_array_add()* function to add the data to the array object. This function takes two arguments, the first is the array's *json_object* variable and the second is *json_object* variable for the data:

```
json_object_array_add( jarray, jelement);
```

The elements are added sequentially, so frequently a loop is used to fetch or generate the values and then use the *json_object_array_add()* function to build the array.

After building the array and packing it with elements, the third and final step is to add the array object to the main JSON data object. The *json_object_object_add()* function is used, just as it is in the preceding sections to add other name/value pairs.

13-04_makearray.c

```
1   #include <stdio.h>
2   #include <stdlib.h>
3   #include <json-c/json.h>
4
5   int main()
6   {
7       json_object *newobj,*jarray,*jelement;
8       const char a_name[] = "hundreds";
9       const char *jstring;
10      int x;
11
12      newobj = json_object_new_object();
13      if( newobj==NULL )
14      {
15          fprintf(stderr,"Unable to create new object\n");
16          exit(1);
17      }
18      puts("New object created:");
19
20      jarray = json_object_new_array();
21      if( jarray==NULL )
22      {
23          fprintf(stderr,"Unable to create array\n");
24          exit(1);
25      }
26
27      for( x=100; x<901; x+=100 )
28      {
29          jelement = json_object_new_int(x);
30          json_object_array_add( jarray, jelement );
31      }
32      json_object_object_add( newobj, a_name, jarray );
33
34      jstring = json_object_to_json_string_ext(
35              newobj,
36              JSON_C_TO_STRING_PRETTY
37              );
```

```
38        puts(jstring);
39
40        return(0);
41    }
```

The main JSON data objects `newobj` is created at Line 12. Line 20 creates the array object, `jarray`.

The *for* loop at Line 27 fills the array object with 9 elements. The `jelement` object is created as an integer value at Line 29, based on the value of looping variable `x`. This object is added to the array `jarray` at Line 30.

It's okay to reuse the *json_object* variable `jelement` in the loop, just as it's okay to re-use any *json_object* variable that's already been added to another object: Refer to the preceding section and the use of the `newdata` *json_object* to add different data types in the sample code `13-03_moredata.c`.

Finally, at Line 32, the array object is added to `newobj`, given the name stored in *char* pointer `a_name`.

Output is generated at Line 38:

```
New object created:
{
  "hundreds": [
    100,
    200,
    300,
    400,
    500,
    600,
    700,
    800,
    900
  ]
}
```

Creating nested objects

An object can be a data type, often referred to as a nested object. To add a JSON object to JSON data you must first build the object, then add it to a parent *json_object* variable.

♦ *It's at this point as a writer where I regret the developer's overuse of the word "object."*

No new functions need to be introduced to create a JSON nested object. Start with the *json_object_new_object()* function to create the object, though this new object won't be the main or "root" object for the data.

Second, create the data type to add to the nested object: integer, double, string, and so on.

Third use the *json_object_object_add()* function to add the data type to the nested object's *json_object* variable. This process repeats for each name/value pair in the nested object.

Finally, use *json_object_object_add()* to add the nested object and all its name/value pair objects to a parent object, such as the root object.

The following code creates a main object `rootobj` under which an `address` object is created. This object has four objects as children: `street`, `city`, `state`, and `zip`. All the child objects are strings.

13-05_objectobject.c

```
1   #include <stdio.h>
2   #include <stdlib.h>
3   #include <json-c/json.h>
4
5   int main()
6   {
7       json_object *rootobj,*adata,*child;
8       const char a_name[] = "address";
9       const char s_name[] = "street";
10      const char s_value[] = "123 Main St.";
11      const char c_name[] = "city";
12      const char c_value[] = "Anytown";
13      const char t_name[] = "state";
14      const char t_value[] = "WY";
15      const char z_name[] = "zip";
16      const char z_value[] = "98765";
17      const char *jstring;
18
19      rootobj = json_object_new_object();
20      adata = json_object_new_object();
21      if( rootobj==NULL || adata==NULL )
22      {
23          fprintf(stderr,"Initialization failure\n");
24          exit(1);
25      }
26
27      /* Create and add child objects */
28      child = json_object_new_string(s_value);
29      json_object_object_add(adata,s_name,child );
30      child = json_object_new_string(c_value);
31      json_object_object_add(adata,c_name,child );
32      child = json_object_new_string(t_value);
33      json_object_object_add(adata,t_name,child );
```

```
34      child = json_object_new_string(z_value);
35      json_object_object_add(adata,z_name,child );
36      /* add adata object to root object */
37      json_object_object_add(rootobj,a_name,adata);
38
39      jstring = json_object_to_json_string_ext(
40              rootobj,
41              JSON_C_TO_STRING_PRETTY
42              );
43      puts(jstring);
44
45      return(0);
46  }
```

Lines 8 through 17 setup the *const char* variables, which I do in this manner primarily to keep the code's line length short so that it doesn't wrap ugly. It's far easier in your own code to use the names directly in a function, such as:

```
child = json_object_new_string((const char *)"WY");
```

The main object, `rootobj`, is obtained at Line 19. This is the top-level JSON data container.

The object `adata` is created at line 20. Like `rootobj`, the *json_object_new_object()* function creates this object.

A series of functions starting at Line 28 creates new string values and then assigns those strings to the `adata` object. Each assignment creates a new name/value pair – a JSON object – associated with the `adata` object.

Finally, at Line 37, the `adata` object is added to the `rootobj` object, creating the nested object. The `adata` object's name is assigned in the *json_object_object_add()* function at Line 37. Here's the output:

```
{
  "address":{
    "street":"123 Main St.",
    "city":"Anytown",
    "state":"WY",
    "zip":"98765"
  }
}
```

Sending data to a file

The counterpart to the *json_object_from_file()* function is *json_object_to_file()*. As you may suspect, it writes a *json_object* to a named file.

The *json_object_to_file()* function requires two arguments: a *const char* string representing the filename and a *json_object* pointer structure representing the data to write.

If the function fails, it returns a value of -1, which you should check for in your code, but I omit in the following example:

13-06_json_write.c

```
1    #include <stdio.h>
2    #include <stdlib.h>
3    #include <json-c/json.h>
4
5    int main()
6    {
7        json_object *rootobj,*adata,*child;
8        const char a_name[] = "address";
9        const char s_name[] = "street";
10       const char s_value[] = "123 Main St.";
11       const char c_name[] = "city";
12       const char c_value[] = "Anytown";
13       const char t_name[] = "state";
14       const char t_value[] = "WY";
15       const char z_name[] = "zip";
16       const char z_value[] = "98765";
17       const char filename[] = "jsontest.json";
18
19       rootobj = json_object_new_object();
20       adata = json_object_new_object();
21       if( rootobj==NULL || adata==NULL )
22       {
23           fprintf(stderr,"Initialization failure\n");
24           exit(1);
25       }
26
27       /* Create and add child objects */
28       child = json_object_new_string(s_value);
29       json_object_object_add(adata,s_name,child );
30       child = json_object_new_string(c_value);
31       json_object_object_add(adata,c_name,child );
32       child = json_object_new_string(t_value);
33       json_object_object_add(adata,t_name,child );
34       child = json_object_new_string(z_value);
35       json_object_object_add(adata,z_name,child );
36       /* add adata object to root object */
37       json_object_object_add(rootobj,a_name,adata);
38
39       json_object_to_file(filename,rootobj);
40       printf("File %s written\n",filename);
41
42       return(0);
43    }
```

This code is based in the preceding example, 13-05_objectobject.c, with the addition of the filename variable at Line 17 and the two statements at Lines 39 and 40. The nested object created is output to the file `jsontest.json`.

Here are the file's contents.

```
{"address":{"street":"123 Main
St.","city":"Anytown","state":"WY","zip":"98765"}}
```

If you want pretty output instead, then use the *json_object_to_json_string_ext()* function as demonstrated through this Chapter to create a prettified string. Then use your C kung fu to save that string to a file: As with any string data, you can use standard I/O functions to output the string.

Index

Also by Dan Gookin

Check out these other titles available by Dan Gookin at the Amazon Kindle store:

Dan Gookin's Guide to Ncurses Programming

Beginning Programming with C For Dummies

Android Phones and Tablets For Dummies

Word 2019 For Dummies

Word 2016 For Professionals For Dummies

PCs For Dummies

Laptops For Dummies

Check out this website for all current titles:

`http://www.wambooli.com/titles/`

www.ingramcontent.com/pod-product-compliance
Lightning Source LLC
Chambersburg PA
CBHW051255050326
40689CB00007B/1205